10/23

NO WONDER THEY CALL IT THE REAL PRESENCE

415-206-1166

Cathun Surin
2003

No Wonder They Call It the Real Presence

Lives Changed by Christ in Eucharistic Adoration

DAVID PEARSON

CHARIS

SERVANT PUBLICATIONS
ANN ARBOR, MICHIGAN

Charis Books is an imprint of Servant Publications especially designed to serve Roman Catholics.

Servant Publications—Mission Statement

We are dedicated to publishing books that spread the gospel of Jesus Christ, help Christians to live in accordance with that gospel, promote renewal in the church, and bear witness to Christian unity.

Servant Publications
P.O. Box 8617
Ann Arbor, MI 48107
www.servantpub.com

Cover design: Brian Fowler, Grand Rapids, Mich.

02 03 04 05 10 9 8 7 6 5 4 3 2 1

Printed in the United States of America
ISBN 1-56955-324-6

Library of Congress Cataloging-in-Publication Data

Pearson, David, 1960-
    No wonder they call it the real presence : true stories of lives
    changed by Christ / David Pearson.
        p. cm.
    ISBN 1-56955-324-6 (alk. paper)
     1. Lord's Supper--Adoration. 2. Catholic Church--Liturgy. I. Title.
    BX2233 .P43 2002
    264'.02036--dc21

                                                      2002005215

CONTENTS

The Assignment

"I am the living bread that came down from heaven ... and the bread that I will give for the life of the world is my flesh."

Jesus Christ, ca. 33 A.D.

The idea for this book came to me while I was traveling with a colleague a few years ago.

I was a reporter on the beat. Steve was there to do some selling. Industry conventions bring together odd travel mates.

We worked for the same magazine, a trade title covering the medical technology industry, though we didn't know much about one another. Back at the office, our respective departments, sales and editorial, had minimal contact.

And that was no accident.

Sales, intent on filling our pages with as many ads as they could squeeze into each issue, found editorial a bit standoffish for their liking. In their eyes, we were sticklers for detail—an annoying bunch of trivia buffs who couldn't get it through our heads that their customers paid both our salaries.

We, secretly seeing ourselves as the Woodwards and Bernsteins of the business press, thought they were out to schmooze us into writing nothing but puff pieces about their hot prospects. As we saw it, if we succumbed to their charms, we risked compromising the integrity of our journalistic objectivity. Why, our very craft was at stake. Couldn't they see that?

Yep, it wasn't so long ago that this Catholic journalist covered shifts in the MRI market as if the fate of the Fourth Estate hung in the balance.

Anyway, we met at the airport, Steve and I, two of a sizable contingent our publisher was sending to this particular conference. The company had asked us to fly together and share a room at the hotel to save a few bucks, so, with an hour to kill at the gate, waiting to board our flight, I figured, Here's a good chance to practice some interdepartmental diplomacy. Maybe pave the way for better relations "going forward."

Well, leave it to me.

I knew things were even more testy than usual, of late, between sales and editorial. I knew Steve and I would be spending the next four days in and out of one another's orbit. I knew that many's the irreparable rift started by small talk. So I should have done all I could to keep the conversation especially light. The weather. Sports. The pros and cons of doing the Macarena at company parties. Anything but politics or religion.

But no. I had to go and ask Steve about the cross he was wearing on his lapel. (Credit where credit is due: At least I refrained from ribbing him about showing up for a six-hour flight in a suit and tie.) The cross had a number "7" where the corpus would be on a Catholic crucifix. What was the significance of that?

Steve didn't know. The person who gave it to him had told him the numeral somehow signified "God's choicest blessings" and, well, that was good enough for him. When it came to religion, Steve said, he only knew two things. One, he loved Jesus and the Bible and all the "positive energy" his faith gave him to succeed in his career and family life. And two, he had no stomach for the Catholic Church.

It was going to be a long four days.

* * * * *

Steve, I quickly learned, was a former Catholic. He had left the Church when he divorced his first wife and married a second. As he talked, it became obvious that his present faith was a singular syncretism of born-again-Christian orthodoxy and New Age, power-of-positive-thinking novelty. "The Lord wants us to realize all our dreams," he explained in an excited whisper, then cited a verse of Scripture to prove it.

Seeing his uncontainable zeal, I figured the best thing to do was to let him know he was talking to a Catholic, then lie low and hear him out. That's what I did and, to his credit, Steve cooled it on the Church and just preached the Gospel According to Steve: Seek health, pursue wealth and give God the glory.

As it turned out, once we boarded our plane, I didn't see a whole lot of Steve. For the rest of the conference, he went his way and I went mine; as for being reluctant roomies, by the time I got in each night, he was already sacked out. (Go figure. I thought *sales* people were the up-all-nighters.)

It wasn't until our final morning at the hotel, while we were both packing our bags, that Steve and I had another chance to chat. He quickly brought up the "R" subject again. It was evident he'd been itching for the opportunity.

We jawed about matters of faith and Christian doctrine a bit, the task at hand providing a convenient distraction and a safe buffer zone. That cracked quickly enough when Steve paused from his packing, put his hands on his hips and said, "Look, I still believe everything the Catholic Church teaches."

"Really?" I asked, feigning credulity as I recalled the wacky theology lesson I'd been treated to at the airport. "Then why'd you leave?"

Visibly perturbed, he shot me a cross look. Then he said something I'll never forget: "Because they say I can't receive the bread of Christ there."

"The what?" I asked, thinking I might have heard wrong. "You mean Communion?"

"Right. Communion. The bread of Christ."

"Steve, where did you hear that term—the *bread* of Christ—for the Eucharist?"

"What? Am I saying something wrong?"

"Actually, you are. It's not his bread. It's his Body. There's a big difference."

"Semantics," said Steve, a familiar facial expression betraying his aggravation with a nit-picking editorial type. "The bottom line," he added as he folded a crisp white shirt and set it in his suitcase just so, "is that the pastors at *my* church don't judge. They give all their blessings, including Communion, to anyone who comes forward with faith. If you ask me, that's what Jesus would do—not what the Catholic Church does."

Yeah, like I possessed the apologetic acumen to cut through that. And without opening up a major interdepartmental rift? *L'impossible.* It was time to shake hands, say I was sorry we saw things from a different point of view and make a mental note to pray in front of the Blessed Sacrament for Steve later.

* * * * *

Looking back, I suspect that, had the conversation proven an isolated incident, I would have forgotten about Steve's small, but telling, blunder in the busy weeks that followed. What ended up burning the exchange into my brain was its timing. For it was right around this period, the mid-1990s, that the mainstream media began splashing a survey of U.S. Catholics in print and broadcast outlets from coast to coast. Among the study's most striking findings: Only a third of the nation's Catholics said they believed Christ is really present in the Eucharist.

And, for me, a Catholic who'd returned to the Church from evangelical Protestantism a few years prior—largely *because of* the Eucharist—this was to become a time when those statistics would begin taking on real faces with real voices, some much closer to home than a coworker on a business trip.

"Jesus is there wherever two or more are gathered in his name. You can't confine him to a particular place and time," insisted a former Catholic in my family who now partakes of pita bread and grape juice every Sunday morning in an independent evangelical church.

"It's the faith you bring to Communion that makes it meaningful to you as an individual," declared a Catholic neighbor.

"*We* are Eucharist," proclaimed a would-be defender of the faith in an anti-Catholic discussion board on the Internet.

Where were the Catholics who knew, believed, understood and, most importantly, *lived*, the Church's teachings on the Eucharist— source and summit of the Christian life, focal point and foundation of true Christian unity?

Where were the rank-and-file Catholics who understood that, ever since the Last Supper, the Eucharist is, was and always will be Jesus Christ—body and blood, soul and divinity?

Where were the Catholic mothers, fathers, sons and daughters who "get it" that, in the Eucharist alone, Jesus is present in his humanity as well as his divinity?

Eventually, after my own prayer time before the Blessed Sacrament led me to leave the business beat for the Catholic press, I set out to look for a few good Catholics. Not just for reassurance, or to make new friends in the faith, but because the sad state of affairs, it seemed to me, screamed for a response. The situation, in other words, begged for a book.

The book you're holding in your hands is the result. And, let me tell you, it's not the book I intended to write.

* * * * *

Initially I planned to combine eucharistic history, theology and apologetics with a few quotes from Catholics who had a decent handle on eucharistic doctrine. The last element would take the most leg work, so that's where I started.

You might say that I never made it out of the chapel. The eucharistic adoration chapel, that is.

Figuring that, if any lay people would know the Eucharist, it would be folks active in eucharistic adoration—silent prayer before the exposed Host—I worked the beat as I would on any story. I put out my feelers, via phone and e-mail, asking my contacts if they knew of any Catholics who had been active in adoration for at least a year and might be willing to talk about their faith with a reporter. I was thrilled when it proved a snap to come up with the names and phone numbers of more than thirty people from around the country who fit that description. Then, trusty tape recorder in hand, I went on "quote reconnaissance," mostly over the phone but visiting some people in person, too.

It was while playing back the tape of my third interview that I realized the history, theology and apologetics could wait for another book. And recognized that God was prompting me not to probe my sources' knowledge of eucharistic doctrine but to record their experiences in, and flowing into their lives from, eucharistic adoration itself.

The more tapes I transcribed, the more moved I was by the quiet power of these randomly chosen individuals' humble Christian witness. Over and over again, I found myself saying, out loud: "What can I possibly add to *this*?"

In other words, I went looking for a few juicy quotes and got witnessed to. Big time.

And that's how I came to compile this series of one-on-one interviews—or "Q & A's," as we call them at the national weekly newspaper for which I work as an editor, the *National Catholic Register* (in which portions of this introduction ran some time back).

The handful of conversations I ended up selecting for inclusion in this book were the ones I thought were the most representative of all the interviews I conducted. Some of the names have been changed, but only minor edits have been made, for the sake of clarity and conciseness, to the exact words spoken.

Read what these folks told me and see if you don't agree that, in the Eucharist, not only did Jesus give the Church its greatest treasure, but also its members their greatest source of spiritual adventure.

Where the world sees a silent person on his or her knees, praying earnestly or thinking deeply, you'll begin to see hearts and souls on an exhilarating interior journey to the very heart of God.

Where many Christians today speak of enjoying a personal relationship with Christ, you'll see Catholics experiencing authentic intimacy with the creator of all existence.

Where psychologists and social scientists scratch their heads over the curious persistence of an ancient religious devotion, you'll see the embrace between God and man at its warmest.

It's my prayer that, in reading these testimonies, you'll hear Jesus calling you to sit a while each week at his side. And that, as you do, you'll pray for the Steves in your life—the Catholics only vaguely aware of what (and whom) it is they receive (or pass up) in weekly Communion, and our brothers and sisters in separated churches, content in their impression that one blessed bread is as nourishing as the next.

After all, that, in a nutshell, is the whole point of living the Eucharist: letting Christ so fill your heart with faith, hope and love for him that telling others about his eucharistic presence is no longer an option. It becomes an irresistible urge.

Here's how Pope John Paul II has put it:

"[A]ll those who receive the Bread of Life know that they are not only indebted to God, but also to one another.... From this flows the joy of witnessing to God's merciful love of the world. Selfishness cannot prevail in those who live in the Eucharist, because Christ dwells within them (cf. Galatians 2:20).

"This interior renewal gives rise to the desire to be open to one's brothers and sisters in order to build together the kingdom of God."

Read on and let these friends in the faith help you to become a better builder.

And see if, after hearing their stories, you don't find yourself saying, along with me: *No wonder they call it the Real Presence.*

CHAPTER 1

Jay

"[T]he Eucharist is the flesh of our Savior Jesus Christ, flesh which suffered for our sins and which the Father, in his goodness, raised up again."

St. Ignatius of Antioch (died ca. 107)

Within a few minutes after Jay answered the phone, I knew I was speaking with someone who in generations past would have been thought of as a "man's man."

A forty-six-year-old husband and father of two college-age children, he holds no less than three positions at the Catholic high school for which he works—history teacher, guidance counselor and track coach. In fact, the latter is a demanding assignment all its own since there are three separate squads to manage—indoors, outdoors and cross-country. All three, he notes matter-of-factly, "just crush everyone." And that's no bluster: His teams have won ten of their state's last twelve championships; the cross-country team was nationally ranked in 2001.

Like the firefighters and police officers who rushed into the burning World Trade Center towers that fateful September morning, here is a man who prefers to communicate his devotion to God through actions rather than words. "Terse" would be too strong a word to describe his responses to my questions, but he certainly got right to the point on each and, once satisfied he had put it across, let it be known by his silence that he was ready for the next question.

If Jay is, in the world's eyes, a throwback to the days of the "strong, silent type," well, I thought that was just one of the qualities that made his eucharistic adoration testimony so convincing and compelling.

"I started going to adoration at the beginning of the year 2000, the Jubilee Year," Jay told me. "It was when the Church was urging everyone to 'Open Wide the Doors to Christ.'"

Prior to that, our pastor had presented the idea of our parish starting perpetual adoration. We had adoration for years, but only one day a week, not perpetual. He was telling us what a good thing this would be for the parish, for the soul of the parish and the souls of individual people in and around the parish.

I found out then that the Blessed Sacrament, when exposed, can never be left unaccompanied. There are 168 hours in a week, and we needed a person committed to each and every one of them. They needed people to step out a little and make a pretty serious commitment in order to make the whole thing work.

I had never done anything like that related to church. I went to Mass on Sundays and that was that. But my wife and I were sitting there and she said, "This would be a good thing for us to do." I said, "Yeah—it might be worth a shot." So we signed up for Wednesday mornings at five and started setting the alarm for four.

We went off our first time and, right off the bat, I just got the sense that this was something that I had been missing out on. I'm not so sure before we started going that I really understood what "Real Presence" meant and what the Eucharist really was. Or who it really is, I guess I should say.

Has eucharistic adoration made any kind of noticeable difference in your life?

The whole thing has gotten me much more involved in my faith and my parish. It's made me look at a lot of things differently. All the pieces of my faith just kind of came together, and I see how important it is to do more than just meet my minimum obligation.

For example, right after we started with perpetual adoration, the guy who runs education for the parish started teaching a class on the Eucharist. So we jumped into that, too. We started studying this book *The Lamb's Supper* by Scott Hahn, which just gave me more to feed on. I started to say, "Wow—this stuff is real. It goes very deep." You know, you pick up a piece here, a piece there, and pretty soon everything starts to come into very clear focus.

What do you know now that you didn't know prior to January of 2000?

One thing is, I've come to see our pastor in a different light. I used to look at him as too good to be true, all wrapped up in what wasn't real. But now that I have a better handle on things, I see that what he's wrapped up in is reality. I have to credit him with bringing eucharistic adoration to us, because that's what has brought the faith alive for me.

When you're at Mass, a lot of times what happens is almost like you become a spectator. You find yourself thinking, "Gee, I hope it's a good sermon. Hopefully he'll throw us something we can chew on today." Now I realize that's not what you're there for. The Word and the preaching are important, but the main thing you're there for, the central point of the Mass, is Jesus Christ, in the flesh. The Eucharist.

As you start seeing that, and how God really works, you see so many graces start coming into your life. Your life changes. It can't help but change.

And one of the most obvious changes is more involvement with your parish.

More involvement and more appreciation. Our parish has very long Masses. They all go at least an hour. I used to spend a lot of time looking at my watch. I never seem to do that anymore.

Another thing I have to point out is that it's more than just getting more out of church. I also find that I love my work more than ever. This is my twenty-fourth year at this school. You take the bad with the good, but there's not a day I don't look forward to going out the door. I really mean that. And I think, again, it all comes back to adoration.

I used to like my work before, but now I just have a whole different feel on it. I just understand better how I'm supposed to be with people. I understand how to be patient with the students and not be in a crabby mood and be a jerk about some of the things they do. Because then all I'm doing is being selfish. And if something is bothering me, I'm not treating them the way Jesus would treat them—or the way he treats me, for that matter. And those are really the things I ask for. I ask for help to be a better follower of Christ, like the Blessed Mother and the saints.

Did praying in silence before the elevated Host come naturally to you, or did it seem a little odd at first?

We share our hour with another couple. The first time we walked into the adoration chapel, I kind of watched a little bit. I wasn't exactly sure what to do. The chapel was very quiet. Not quiet like a library, but peaceful on a much deeper level. I knew it was a unique place and unlike any place I'd been before. I just started saying my prayers; it seemed like the right thing to do.

Little by little I have kind of developed some strategies, different things I do to stay focused. But that first time I went in, I remember picking up one of the books they have in there. *An Hour With Jesus*, I think it was called. Little meditations. I remember reading the first one I opened to. It said something like, "What would happen if the president came in? Or a movie star or a sports hero? The place would be packed. And yet here you are with the Lord, and there's just you and a couple of other people to greet him"—something to that effect.

I remember reading that and thinking, "That's interesting." So little by little you get into these things. You sit, you maybe do a little reading. I've got a bunch of books I'm reading now that I never would have even picked up before. I've got one on the Blessed Mother, one on the Eucharist, one on the life of Christ.

Has your spiritual life in general developed along with your devotion to Christ in the Eucharist?
Oh, yeah. It's kind of branched out from adoration. I'll give you an example. Last spring, we were encouraged to do the total consecration to Mary according to the writings of St. Louis de Montfort. Near the end of his book, there's a suggestion to pledge to do something special, as part of your consecration, for God. Something maybe a little sacrificial, or at least a little out of your way. I thought about it and I asked myself, "What can I do? There's got to be something meaningful that I can do."

Finally I decided to go before the Blessed Sacrament every day. And that's in addition to my weekly hour of adoration, not to replace it. Every day, I stop in for a least a few minutes. It doesn't have to be the adoration chapel at the parish; it could be the chapel at school or any Catholic church. The Eucharist doesn't have to be exposed; it's OK if it's reserved in the tabernacle. The bottom line is that I'm spending time near the Blessed Sacrament every single day.

And how is that going?

So far, so good. It's been two months and I haven't missed a day yet. That doesn't make me St. Francis, but it's a commitment, a connection.

What do you do in those visits?

Pretty much the same thing that I do in my hour of adoration; it's just condensed. In the daily visits, as in weekly adoration, I try to always start by saying the short prayer St. Francis used to have the brothers say whenever they walked into a church or chapel: "We adore you, Lord Jesus Christ, here and in all your churches in the whole world, and we bless you, because by your holy cross you have redeemed the world."

Then I say some short prayers. And then I always ask for the same three things. I ask to be more faithful, more hopeful and more charitable. Then I say an Our Father and three Hail Marys—one each for greater faith, hope and love, the theological virtues. That's really what I spend most of my time working on.

In adoration, I usually spend fifteen or twenty minutes, kneeling, in that kind of prayer. The rest of the hour, I'll sit and either read or listen as best I can. I have an attention-span problem; I don't do very well with the rosary. In place of that, I'll sometimes think about how I can do better on the Blessed Mother's graces, which St. Louis lists in his book.

How do you know that's really Jesus up there, coming to you under the appearance of bread?

Well, I hope I know. As I said, one of the main things I pray for is more faith. Because sometimes you do catch yourself doubting. I won't deny that. After all, we're fallen people in a fallen world. Our tendency is to trust our feelings rather than our faith.

When I catch myself sliding into those doubts, I remind myself: Hey, the Church has been proclaiming for two thousand years, since the day Jesus went up into heaven before their very eyes, that the Eucharist is Jesus—body and blood, soul and divinity. The same Jesus who was born in Bethlehem, who taught the elders in the temple when he was just a boy, who picked the apostles, who did all the miracles, who died on the cross and rose from the dead—this is not a different Jesus. It's the same one.

At those moments I also like to recall something I learned recently, something that really strikes a chord for me because I'm a history teacher. One of the main reasons the Romans threw the early Christians to the lions was because they thought the Christians were cannibals. They heard they were eating the body of Jesus in their assemblies, which of course later came to be called Holy Mass, and they, the Romans, were disgusted by it. They thought it was a sick, pagan, cannibalistic ritual.

And the Christians—rather than deny that's what their gathering was all about, the Christians stood firm in their faith all the way to torture and martyrdom. They said, "Yes, we are eating the Body of Christ." The saints and martyrs throughout the past twenty centuries have said the same. I'm in no position to argue with that kind of witness.

Going back even further, to the sixth chapter of St. John's Gospel, you have Jesus giving his Bread of Life discourse. Where he insists that his disciples must eat his flesh and refuses to say he's speaking metaphorically when they press him on it, it's the only record Scripture gives of his followers forsaking him for a purely doctrinal reason. John shows it was a teaching a lot of them just would not accept. Then, of course, there's the Last Supper, and in Luke's

Gospel, you have the disciples on the road to Emmaus. It was just after the Resurrection and they didn't recognize Jesus until he broke the bread, blessed it and gave it to them. St. Luke went out of his way to show the connection between the consecrating of the bread and the disciples' recognition of the risen Christ.

Exactly. And that's how we are in adoration. We only recognize him through our faith, if we have faith that it is him because the Church has always taught it.

You know, I've checked and I'm satisfied that the Church is right in its teachings in everything else. I don't think it would be wrong on its single, central, most important teaching.

And I also think, how lucky were those people who actually got to see him and be with him in the flesh. And then I realize, well, I'm even luckier. I get to see him in the flesh, too. And to meditate on his words, "Blessed are they who have not seen, and yet believe."

Jay, you strike me as someone who maybe wouldn't have expected to find himself having such a rich religious experience. Today you might be what you, yourself, would have considered, not so long ago, a "religious fanatic." Am I right?

Well, I've definitely had a religious conversion. And it's ongoing; the Church teaches that your conversion to Christ is a lifelong process, not a one-time event.

Sometimes I am surprised by this turn of events, if I stop and think about it, but it's been such a good, positive thing that I have no reason to look at it from that point of view.

You know, at school we pray before class. It used to be a perfunctory Our Father. You got it out of the way and moved on. But now I feel like prayer really matters. Not only to me but to the students. I can see them more open to the prayers I lead than they used to be. They have strong authenticity detectors; they can easily spot the difference between faith and rote.

Was your faith beginning to revitalize before you signed up for eucharistic adoration? Or did you get involved because your faith life had become sort of a dry duty?

I don't think I was a lot different from most "cradle Catholics," those of us who were baptized as infants and grew up with the faith. You made your confirmation, then you went to Sunday Mass and didn't think too much about it. You had that base covered. You took it all for granted.

As an adult, you're always looking for something that's going to help you get a little more out of your faith. And I know that what you get out of something is in direct proportion to how much you put into it. So, sure, I was looking to get more out of my faith. I thought, well, this eucharistic adoration will strengthen me as a Catholic; this will move me forward somehow.

And now you're a stronger Christian as a result of your devotion.

Well, I'm there in a church or chapel every single day. That would have been unthinkable for me before. I wouldn't have thought I could keep such a commitment. I have a very busy schedule being a father and a husband, plus my work teaching and coaching. And yet I now feel like something essential would be missing from my life if not for my time spent with Christ.

I was so busy today at school, but I wanted to get my five-minute visit to Christ in. I went into the school chapel. The Eucharist is not exposed there, but it's reserved in a beautiful little tabernacle. Today, like a lot of times when I go in there, I'm the only one there. And that's really nice because you can pray out loud. And I go right up front, get right up close, kneel on the carpet, touch the tabernacle and just talk to Jesus. It's very beautiful.

What kinds of changes have you seen in your relationships with other people since you started eucharistic adoration?

I've seen changes in me, and that affects the way I interact with other people. With my family, my wife and children, things have always been pretty good. But with my sisters—you know, in a family you have problems, people not talking to one another or whatever. When something happens, nobody really calls each other to clear the air. It just hangs over everyone for a long time. Well, it seems now that I'm always the one who gives in and calls. And they'll always say, "I'm really glad you called."

I have one sister who never talks to any of us. And she never returns calls even if you try to reach out to her. But lately I've been calling her and leaving messages for her, just to let her know that I'm there and I care. One of these days, whatever funk she's in, she'll come out of it. But that isn't going to happen if no one talks to her or reaches out to her.

Now, before, I would have taken the attitude, "Well, I'll show her. She's not talking to me? Well I'll *never* talk to *her*." And I would have made good on it, too. I was talking about the situation to my other sister just the other day. I said, "I've been leaving her messages because this is what we have to do to try to make things better." I heard myself saying that and said to myself, "Isn't that interesting? I never used to say stuff like that."

Have you received answers to any specific prayer requests you've made in adoration?

There have been situations I've brought to the Lord in adoration where the prayers have just *clearly* been answered. I've prayed about kids at school with problems, kids who have incredibly bad situations at home and so on. A couple of these situations have improved dramatically.

One kid had school phobia. He would not come to school. He was paralyzed with fear. So I brought that before Jesus in the adoration chapel, then counseled the kid, along with our school chaplain. We did some very intensive counseling for quite a while; it was kind of a hard case. And the kid is fine now. He comes to school. I saw him at a dance the other night.

And by the way, I prayed for him but not so much with him. I perceived that he wasn't too comfortable with that yet. So I did more praying for him than with him.

You and your wife go to adoration together. Has it strengthened your marriage?

I think it's made a big difference. Because we go to adoration together, there's that common bond. It's unspoken, for the most part, but it's there.

After we made our consecration and I started making daily visits to the Blessed Sacrament, I realized one night that I hadn't yet been that day. I said, "Listen, I'm going to go to the chapel for a short while." I reminded her about my commitment to make daily visits to the Blessed Sacrament. And she said, "I'll go with you." So we went and spent about twenty minutes. And she asked me, "So this is your little personal deal? This is what you do?" And I said, "This is it. It's just something I wanted to do." And she said, "I think it's a good thing."

So it's kind of moved us closer to the same wavelength, spiritually. It's a common reference point at the center of each of our lives. I'm not going to say that our marriage is suddenly perfect, because none is, but our eucharistic devotion certainly has added a positive dimension that wasn't there before.

Our pastor, when he started this program, and he was explaining it to us, he said, "For those of you who get involved, things will never be the same." Soon after we started, after we had gone a couple of Wednesdays, I told the chaplain at school about our involvement with adoration at our parish. I couldn't believe it when he said the exact same words: "Things will never be the same for you." The exact same words.

I remember that now because they were both right. Things are definitely not the same. The whole experience just keeps getting better.

CHAPTER 2

Mary

"[J]ust as by God's word Jesus Christ our savior became flesh and blood for our salvation, so also we have been taught that the food made Eucharist by the word of prayer that comes from him is both the flesh and the blood of that Jesus who was made flesh."

St. Justin Martyr (died ca. 165)

I was awestruck by Mary's selfless concern for others in light of what she had just been through herself.

Diagnosed with cancer in early 2001, the forty-three-year-old went through months of painful chemo- and radiation therapy. Along with the usual hair loss, nausea and weakness that always accompany such treatments, she also had to endure chronic insomnia, severe bruising and an excruciating infection in her gums (the result of an abscessed wisdom tooth and a suppressed immune system). She was still struggling to get back to normal, physically and emotionally, when we spoke.

Yet, despite all her suffering, she was eager to witness the power of Christ in eucharistic adoration—and she could not conceal what was foremost on her mind: her ten-year-old son, who was lately evidencing symptoms of a developmental disorder.

Mary told me how, years earlier, she had gone away to college to escape the despair of an alcoholic father. How she had stopped practicing her faith at that time, even though she was at a solid Catholic school, because of years of unanswered prayers on his behalf. How she graduated near the top of her class, married a dutiful Catholic who never missed Mass on Sunday, had three children with him. How she worked as a dietician in several mental health hospitals even as she hoped work would open up in a more prestigious, university medical center. ("I couldn't understand why God wasn't opening 'the right doors' for me.")

Then she described how, when her husband's booming business went through a series of financial reversals, and it looked as though they might lose everything in their secure suburban world, she turned back to God for "help, hope and answers."

And she told me how a profound conversion experience followed, thanks largely to a charismatic prayer group she joined, with much skepticism and trepidation, at their parish. How she came to realize her work in mental health facilities was preparation for what she would go through, years later, with her son.

And how, when the parish instituted perpetual eucharistic adoration several years ago, she literally leapt for joy.

"I go to that chapel at two or three in the morning, sometimes in the midst of a bout of insomnia, where I may not have had sleep for four or five nights in a row," she says. "I sit there and Jesus gives me what I need to get through it. Even when I'm in total darkness of the soul, where I have no idea what's going on with my child, I know some answer will come. It always has."

It sounds as if your son's emotional problems are your main concern even though you, yourself, are at the tail end of a long fight with cancer. Well, the cancer is beaten. It actually seems like a long time ago, even though you can still see some of the effects of the chemotherapy. At this point, I really think the cancer was just a springboard God used to prepare me to help my son and maybe my husband's family, where there are also some mental health issues. And who knows who else?

Cancer is a scary six-letter word, though. Did the diagnosis send you into the chapel?
Oh, yeah. But I was already there anyway, very committed to adoration, at the time of the diagnosis. I had been involved with regular, scheduled adoration for about a year. A year before that, when they announced that they were going to establish perpetual adoration at our parish, I had been praying for just that so I could get to it more often than just during the day. Prior to that, we had an adoration chapel, but it was only open certain hours during the day. For a while, perpetual just didn't seem to get going. Finally, when they decided that they were really going to make it happen, they closed the chapel for a while to paint it, refurbish and so on.

My best friend and I both had kids in school, so we would drive to find adoration chapels all over the region. We were like adoration junkies! Because when life is really giving you a lot of trouble, you go straight to adoration and it gives you that hour of supernatural, transcendent peace in the presence of Jesus. You can't live there forever, but you wish you could. You wish you could stay and never come out.

Then the chapel reopened, this time for perpetual adoration.
Right. The bishop came, led a very beautiful liturgy and put Jesus in our chapel. We could come adore Jesus closer to home. After daily Mass first thing in the morning, you can go straight to the chapel and it just brings you such strength and such clear answers to your problems. You just know you're not going to get that kind of direction, that kind of assurance, by going through other channels. Self-help groups

and all these things, whether they're for cancer survivors or parents of children with special needs—you don't need those things if you have access to Jesus in adoration whenever you need him. All you need to do is go to the chapel, sit there and let him work. He can solve so many problems. You have to be patient, though. I've learned that. The answers don't always come right away.

How was it that you came to take on such a difficult hour?
I volunteered for 3 A.M. right at the beginning. I knew that those wee hours of the morning are the most precious because you are really there alone with Jesus, often in perfect, silent stillness. I'm also captain of the 3 A.M. slot, which means I make sure that hour is covered all seven days of the week. I thought it would be tough to fill, but it's been very easy. It turns out lots of people love the stillness of that hour, just as I do.

At first my husband wasn't crazy about my leaving the house at that hour, especially during the [cancer] treatments. He felt I was too weak. He really pressed the issue, so I found a substitute. But now I'm getting back to it and he's OK with that. He hasn't exactly been enthusiastic about it, but he knows how much it means to me so he kind of stays quiet about it.

When you were diagnosed with cancer, you were already dealing with your son's behavioral problems, plus serious financial concerns. What did you pray about when you had so much to pray about?
Well, this may shock you, but I actually thought maybe God was offering me a way out. I mean, through death. I had been reading St. Thérèse of Lisieux and I remember being struck by her response to her tuberculosis when her body really started to break down. She took her vomiting of blood as her ticket to heaven. That's how I started to

think. Like, "I am out of here; God's going to call me home to him and out of this mess." And I was actually planning on refusing treatment, which was sending my family into a crisis. They were devastated. They thought I was crazy, depressed and a nut.

I kept saying to myself, this is God giving me a choice. I can go and be with him, or I can stay here. I had to go through a discernment process as to whether I should take treatment or not. And, going through it, he let me know that I should stay down here and be a good wife and mother.

So I discerned that choice, though it's not like I don't still have days where I say, "I could have been out of here!" I know how selfish that sounds, but it would have been an honorable way to go home. It didn't involve divorce or betrayal; God was giving me the option. St. Paul, of course, prayed pretty much the same thing, so I knew I was in good company. I didn't feel guilty about wanting to go home to be with Jesus.

Was eucharistic adoration an important part of your discernment on this?
It was the main thing, the place where I most clearly heard God's call to my heart to stay here.

One of the ways he reached me was by directing me to specific Scriptures. I would go into the chapel and say, "OK, God, you've got to speak to me and tell me flat-out because that's the only way I can be reached. I'm not good at putting together little clues or deciphering poetic verses of Scripture; you need to really hit me over the head with what you want me to do." Then I would sort of randomly open my Bible and, time after time, I would come to a verse or a section that really spelled out that I belonged down here doing my work as a mother and a wife. I needed to go through with the treatments.

It was just very obvious that he was saying: "I'm not calling you to heaven, Mary. I'm calling you right where you are. Trust me; have faith in me. What I will ask will be simple. I'll do the work; all you need to do is pray and trust."

So that's exactly what I've been doing, and God has made good on his promises. Not only has my relationship with my husband improved, and not only have we been unified over needing to seek out professional help for our son, but other things, too. For example, God has changed our teenager from wanting absolutely nothing to do with the Church to joining a very devout youth group at the parish.

There are other things, so many answered prayers. It's so obvious the Lord is working in our family, and eucharistic adoration is sort of the epicenter of the whole thing. My husband and children may not see that, but I do.

What's your routine in adoration?

I come in the door at about 2:45 A.M. I genuflect, I ask for blessings and the grace to clear my mind of all distractions, and just concentrate on praying. Whatever is bothering me or distracting me, I'll bring to Jesus. Then I sit down or kneel and I pray the rosary. And that settles me down. The rhythm, the concentration, the focus, settles my heart rate right down. I pray whichever set of mysteries I'm moved to pray that morning, the joyful, sorrowful or glorious mysteries of Christ's life.

Then I sit down, think about what's bothering me and say, "Lord, please talk to me about this." And he'll give me a Bible passage, sometimes by moving me to open randomly or page through, other times by a reading from Mass that day or a section I've been studying, and I'll write it down. If it's not super clear at that point what he's trying to say to me, then it's not meant to be—yet, at least. It may become clear later, a few days or even weeks from then as it sinks in and I pray about it. But when I really need a clear answer on something, he always comes through with one.

And then I put the Bible down and I think about it. And, if it's simple and direct, I just ask myself what I'm supposed to do to put the answer in action. Other times, I'll pick out a book from the shelves we have in our chapel—we have lots of great books on spirituality, the Catechism, saints' lives and so on. And I'll stick with that book, a little at a time each week, until I'm done with it. And I finish my hour, give my thanksgiving and then go home.

When I'm in trouble, beyond the ability even to focus my thoughts really well, I'll go in and just sit. I might tell Jesus I need his peace in my heart, then just sit with him in silence for a long time. When something good happens, I sometimes come in and say, "Thank you, thank you, thank you!" Just spend the whole hour giving thanks to God.

It sounds as if eucharistic adoration has changed you, your family and your whole parish.
More than I can describe. It's amazing how God works in the lives not only of those who adore him but also of the people around them.

I've become very close to three other women at our parish. We get together for Scripture study, prayer, the rosary and sometimes just coffee and conversation. And what we all have in common is eucharistic adoration. God took these four women who, between us, have gone through everything, it seems. From childhood traumas to teenage rebellion, broken homes, really wild and dissolute lives in early adulthood, and now to be washed clean by Jesus in the sacraments and striving to live holy lives—it really is amazing how the four of us wound up here, together, united in our Catholic faith.

So, yes, lots of change has come through eucharistic adoration.

What about your relationships within your family, the family you grew up in? Have you seen any changes there?

My brother walked away from the Church and married outside it. And now he can't find a church home that satisfies him. I tell him: What you're missing is the real presence of Jesus in the Blessed Sacrament. And he just kind of looks at me like, "Oh, that can't be it." I say, "Trust me." He knows, deep in his heart, that I'm right. He's not the kind to listen to someone else; he has to find things out on his own.

My father died two years ago of lung cancer. But not before he got right with God and had an amazing encounter with Jesus in the Blessed Sacrament.

I'm settled here in the Northeast; my folks are back in the Midwest, where I grew up. My father's health had been deteriorating and, when it looked like it was getting near the end, I flew out to help my mother hospice him. When I got there, I found their parish had a priest who was very, very eucharistic. And I'm a eucharistic minister; I can distribute Communion if a priest chooses to send me. Well, this priest allowed me to go to daily Mass and bring Communion to my father, who had returned to the faith soon after his diagnosis came through, after being away from it for many, many years. Remember, most of his life he had been a severe alcoholic.

When his diagnosis came through, I had talked my mom into having the courage to try to steer him back to the Church. His initial reaction was, not surprisingly, "I have sinned so much, God could not forgive me." To make a long story short, he was open to listening because he knew he didn't have long to live—the doctors gave him a zero percent chance of beating this cancer.

So my mother invited this priest, the very eucharistic one, to the house to talk with my dad. I was there at that time, too. The priest was very warm and very enthusiastic about the faith and I said to my mother, "Mom, let's go out for a while." We left my dad there with the priest and, sure enough, by the time we got back, he had made a full, general confession—right there in his own home. It was as though all those prayers I had said throughout my childhood and college years had suddenly been answered, so beautifully, right before my eyes.

Just like that, he was back with the Church and, from then on, he never missed Sunday Mass. So when I returned near the end, when he could no longer leave the house, the only thing that bothered me was how many years he had missed receiving Jesus. And God answered that, too: Because this priest was so eucharistic and I was a eucharistic minister, I was able to get permission to go to daily Mass at their parish, then bring my dad Communion every single day until he could no longer swallow it.

The day before he was going to go to a nursing home—my mother and I couldn't handle caring for him any more at home—the priest gave me two hosts in the pyx. I came home, and my father couldn't even take a piece of it. So I left it there with him. So in the Eucharist, Jesus was in that household the whole time we went through the worst part of my father's cancer.

I look back now and I just know that Christ wanted me to know that he was eucharistically present in my parents' household in those dark hours. I remember getting up in the middle of the night and opening up the pyx to pray to Jesus, so incredibly close to us, through this providential turn of events, in the Blessed Sacrament.

Then, on the day my dad died, I knew it was the day. I got in the car at around four in the morning and drove to the hospital. I had a prayer book with me; it included prayers for the dying. I knelt on the floor of his hospital room and I prayed as long as I could. Then I had to go back and get my mother. It was while I was on my way to get my mother that he died. Later, I thought back to the look on his face when I had left him there to get my mother. He was clearly at peace.

I ended up taking Communion from that pyx that day. That whole chapter in my life was very powerful and reassuring. I was so blessed with the way Jesus put all those pieces together so my dad could die so peacefully, and so I was able to adore Jesus and receive him, in the grace of such extraordinary intimacy, in the darkest hours when I needed him most.

Is your life today ordered around the Eucharist?
It's ordered around Holy Mass, every day. That's the most powerful form of prayer on earth. Eucharistic adoration has helped me center my life on the Mass, but the Mass is a much higher form of prayer than adoration.

How has your eucharistic devotion to Jesus, in adoration and the Mass, changed your prayer life, your spirituality?
My life is more peaceful even though the trials are greater. Through the Eucharist, Jesus gives you answers in a much more simple and direct way than any other avenue. He keeps you on the right path—the path to him.

This is the greatest gift he could give, because it's very difficult to stay on the path to God right now. Even in the wake of the terrible tragedies of the terrorist attacks on our country, when you would think we might wise up at last, there is still so much garbage out there to fill your mind with sinful or unholy things. Even if you, yourself, are pretty well disciplined, you have others to take into account. Your kids are saying, "We want to go to this movie; we want to watch this TV show." And you watch this stuff, and it's absolutely gonzo. You get to where you realize, as you're trying to draw your kids away from that sort of stuff, how very much they—and you—really do need prayer.

It's hard to stay close to God right now, maybe harder than it's ever been. Sometimes it seems as if it takes a heroic effort just to keep your faith in the face of such godlessness and temptations to turn away from him.

These kinds of struggles call for the intercession of the Blessed Mother. Her prayers to God on our behalf are so much more powerful than we'll ever know. She'll take care of this whole area of your life for you; she'll set up your house. She may need to break the TV so you get only two channels, neither of which your kids like [laughs], but she will take care of these things.

You obviously have a very strong devotion to the Blessed Mother. Do you invoke her intercession while adoring Jesus in the eucharistic chapel?
Sure. Why wouldn't I? We worship and adore Jesus, who is God, and we venerate and ask for prayers from Mary—whom he created daughter of God the Father, mother of God the Son and spouse of God the Holy Spirit.

There's a practical side to Marian devotion, too. A lot of times, you're in situations in which you can't relate to a male as well as a female. You want to go to your mother. You want your mom! Well, you can go to your mom. And Jesus is right there with her the whole time. He went to her, too. If she's good enough for Jesus, she's certainly good enough for me.

As a mother and a wife, I know that, to live in a more gentle manner, I need a motherly example sometimes. Jesus, after all, handled things in a masculine way. To see how to handle things in a home, nurturing children and all, you go to the mother. Mary did everything in a very gentle, docile, feminine way.

One of the things I've heard people say is that adoring Jesus in the Eucharist makes a person more sensitive to just how vulnerable Jesus made himself through the Incarnation, and continues to make himself through the Blessed Sacrament. Is that true for you? Definitely. While I was still very sinful, doing all the wrong things, I was going to daily Mass. Christ never once distanced himself from me all during those times. In fact, I would say, as I look back, the graces were strongest when I was getting into the most trouble, morally speaking.

The bottom line is, Jesus has called and people have responded, in however small a way, or else they wouldn't be there at all. He calls sinners—that's exactly whom he does call. Sometimes he has to scale away a lot of stuff to get people to open their eyes to him and their ears to his call to holiness. That's probably more true today than ever, as we said before.

In the Mass, Jesus is really calling. We have to pray for those people who are receiving especially unworthily. They need to get to sacramental confession, but you can't just walk up to them and bark it or you'll drive them away from the Church altogether. You have to pray for them and wait for the right time to witness to them gently. Find out what it is that draws them to Mass, and build on that. It's not my place to judge. And I'm not going to get in Jesus' way. He called them, they responded, so who am I?

Now if they walk up and start talking to me about the specifics of their situation, how they're living with their boyfriend or whatever, I might see that as a sign Jesus is giving to me that he does want me to talk very directly about their situation. And that has certainly happened. But more often than not, I find myself praying for people much more than preaching to them. I'm not called to be a John the Baptist.

Being such a broken vessel myself, who am I to judge? We are all broken vessels. And he works in different lives in different ways. If he's bringing serious sinners to Sunday Mass, well, Hallelujah! At least for that one hour they're docile, in some way, to God.

Do you feel as though your time in adoration is a retreat *from* the world or an entry more deeply *into* it?
Sometimes you go there to retreat, sometimes you know you have to suffer in order to bring about transformation in yourself. You're always working on changing yourself, to make yourself more holy and more pleasing to God, so that others around you can come to Jesus through you. You find you have so many deep-seated prejudices that stop you from being the window to Jesus that you're supposed to be for them. And he has to continually transform you.

We come to him so broken that, in order for him to work through us to reach the next person, he has to completely transform us. I don't know about anyone else, but I'm stubborn. I have to be brought through quite a bit of suffering before I begin to change. God really has to whack me over the head with a two-by-four.

What's been the best, or most rewarding, aspect of eucharistic adoration for you?
The most beautiful thing about a relationship with our eucharistic Lord is that you can just keep going deeper and deeper in love. It's

NO WONDER THEY CALL IT THE REAL PRESENCE

deeper than any mortal person could ever go with you. I don't know how God can do that, but he does. He can just take you deeper and deeper and deeper. The more you learn, the more you don't know. You can just never plumb the depths of God's love and wisdom.

Now you raise a serious theological question: Won't we be bored in heaven? If we have the full beatific vision—no longer seeing God through a glass, dimly, but seeing him face to face, unobstructed—then isn't the mystery of life solved? Isn't our ultimate love requited?

Well, I don't know how to frame the answer in theological terms, but I do know that you can never get tired of loving God.

I think theologians would say something like, Because love is inseparable from truth, there is an intellectual component to loving God: his mind. In other words, he is infinitely interesting, intellectually stimulating if you will, to us, his creatures. For those reasons, we'll never tire of discovering God in heaven.

You said it. The only thing I can add to that is, whether you're intellectual or not, you can never get tired of loving and discovering God.

Meanwhile, however, down here on planet Earth, you do reach a point where the honeymoon kind of ends, don't you? I mean, when your close relationship with God is no longer new, exciting, revelatory.

Yes. Every honeymoon comes to an end, even the one you go on with God when your experience of conversion is new and fresh. I've certainly been through that.

How did you deal with it? What made you persevere when the consolations and sweetness seemed to be drying up?

Well, until you're disciplined, God is either going to send you suffering or put you in situations that are going to keep drawing you back. If you pray, "Please don't let me be drawn away from your eucharistic heart, no matter where my feelings and emotions want to lead me," he won't.

Whatever happens to you is for your own good. Sometimes you have to look back to see that; you can't see the answers while you're living through the questions. As soon as you make that decision to trust—no, you don't even have to trust; all you have to do is make that act of faith that says you *want* to trust—you are headed for trials. Guaranteed, your faith will be tried. And the trials are going to be for your growth and development in Christ. That's just part of an authentic personal relationship with him.

When you get through various trials—when you emerge to the other side and they seem to be behind you—then you can start to see what God was doing. But you almost never see that very clearly while you're in the trial. Just live it, go through it, persevere. And he will be there for you before, during and after.

If you're having a dead, dry prayer life, pray about it. Ask for the grace of prayer. He will give it to you. Whatever you need, just go before the Blessed Sacrament and ask for it. Then don't be surprised when it comes to you. If you're drier than dust, just keep going in and hammering at the rock, waiting for the water to flow. It worked for Moses, it's worked for me, and I can assure you, it will work for anyone.

CHAPTER 3

Dylan

"Do not regard the bread and wine as simply that, for they are, according to the Master's declaration, the body and blood of Christ. Even though the senses suggest to you the other, let faith make you firm."

St. Cyril of Jerusalem (315–86)

It was while speaking with nineteen-year-old Dylan over the phone that I realized the quotes I had begun gathering from my live sources were more than just one set of elements I could incorporate in a book about eucharistic adoration: The quotes were a book in their own right.

I don't think this impressive young man, a convert and a seminarian, needs any more introduction than that.

You're in minor seminary as you earn your undergraduate degree at a Catholic college. What role does eucharistic adoration play in your life?
I spend an hour a day in chapel. Plus, every Thursday, we have exposition and benediction of the Blessed Sacrament.

How long have you been keeping up with an hour a day before the Blessed Sacrament?
Well, it's kind of weird because I'm a convert to the Church. I only became a Catholic as of Easter 1999. And I'd have to say that adoration

is really one of the big reasons I entered the Church. I had never heard of adoration—I came upon it while I was kind of probing the faith.

Ever since I was a young child, I always had sort of a passion, I guess you would call it, for God. But no one in my family was religious at all. So it was always a very personal thing to me. I never even talked to my closest friends about it until recently. So there was a conversion going on for me, though I didn't know at the time what you would call it.

Did you pray even though you had no religious training?
Yes. I would often find myself praying. In fact, there was a Catholic church near my house, and I used to go in there to pray. It's funny now, but I used to go and kneel before the tabernacle without know-ing what was inside. I would look at it and wonder what was in there. And I would wonder what everything around me in the church was all about. When I was in junior high, I began to read the Bible very seri-ously, and to read the lives of the saints. I think I started with Francis of Assisi.

From there I moved on to Church history. The documents of the Second Vatican Council—stuff not on your typical ninth-grader's reading list. I had a real hunger. I never told anyone I was reading these things. It remained very personal; my family didn't even know. And I went to a very intellectually proud public high school, where it really wouldn't have been too cool to let people know that you were delving into religion of any kind.

But it was the Eucharist, really, that ultimately drew me to the Catholic Church—the truth that the Church teaches about the Eucharist. I had started attending Mass, and I heard about eucharistic adoration over the Internet. So I started going to it at a local parish. It was just an informal way to get involved with the Church.

Was your family completely "un-churched"?

Yes. We didn't go to church at all, or even talk much about religion. By the time I went to high school, and started really deepening in my knowledge of the teachings of the Church, all through my own research, I had begun going to church on my own. Usually I would go to the cathedral in the morning, before school, and just pray. Sometimes I would say a rosary, which I learned how to say through a little pamphlet.

Along with private visits to the church, you also went to Mass?

Yes. I was at a parish for one year and then the altar servers asked me to be an altar server. I confessed to them that I wasn't a Catholic, which surprised them because I had been sitting in the front pew for about a year. [Laughs.] I guess they didn't notice, or didn't mind, that I wasn't receiving Communion. And then the priest heard that I wasn't Catholic, and he signed me up for RCIA. I went through that and, finally, became Catholic.

You didn't feel the priest was pushing you into conversion, did you?

Oh, no, absolutely not. I had been coming to his parish for a whole year before he even approached me. And it was something I wanted to do, but I was afraid of jumping too hastily into something I knew was a very serious commitment. Because once you accept baptism, that's when it all starts. I had some apprehension about that—not because I didn't believe but because, on a faith level, I just wanted to make sure I would be able to live up to my baptismal promises. And that is now my home parish.

Let's leap ahead to when you first heard about eucharistic adoration.

Well, the reason I was going to that particular parish was because, on the first Sunday of each month, they would have a Holy Hour. And the Holy Hour I really became attached to, because within the Holy Hour there was an opportunity for silent prayer before Jesus exposed in the Eucharist. I think I've always been somewhat contemplative, so that was very appealing to me. So I had been going to these Holy Hours regularly, as a time for more meditative prayer outside of Mass.

Then the parish instituted all-day adoration one day a week, on Wednesdays. I began going to that as well. So before you knew it, I was going to adoration twice a week.

When you first started going, did it not seem strange to you to be praying before what appeared to be a piece of bread?

You have to remember that I had been reading Scripture and Church history since I was a child. Through my own research, I had come to know the eucharistic theology of the Church. And so it was something I just kind of went with. A lot of people, including some in my own family, continue to question it. But for me it was something I just always accepted; I felt a great reverence for the Eucharist right away. In fact, I don't ever remember thinking of it as a piece of bread. Although, thinking back, maybe I should have—I might have even greater appreciation for it now.

But I always had been reverent toward the Eucharist. It was something, especially at benediction, with the intense prayers and the incensing and all—it was just kind of natural to see people adoring Jesus. I knew that they believed this was Jesus, so kneeling and showing reverence before it seemed like the proper thing to do.

Devil's advocate question: A secular social scientist or religious historian would say you're practicing transcendental meditation with a visual mantra instead of a verbal one—a wafer of unleavened bread in place of an "Om." How do you know that the consecrated Host is the body and blood, soul and divinity of the Jesus who walked the dusty streets of Galilee two thousand years ago?

When you go to adoration, you're making an act of faith. It's a credo. Just by going you're making an act of faith. I guess you could say that, when you make the act of faith, it's like—I don't know who said it, but—"To those who believe, no explanation is necessary; to those who do not believe, no explanation is sufficient."

I don't know what I'd respond to the devil's advocate, but I do know that going to adore Jesus is an act of faith in and of itself. And when you learn what the Eucharist is, and when you pray before the Eucharist, you are filled with graces. It's supernatural. It's something that a scientist can't quantify. It's not something you can demonstrate empirically. It happens on a higher level, where faith accepts what reason cannot comprehend. You can study the theology behind it—it's very deep and very beautiful—but if you choose not to believe, you won't believe.

For me, I just realize I'm in the physical presence of God. I think when you're in the act of adoring him, because you're performing an act of faith, you're fostering a deeply personal relationship with him. In fact, I don't think "personal" is the right term; I think "intimate" is probably more accurate. And there are merits you begin to discover in your life as a result. And there's really not a reason to question, because you understand the one you love better just by making that act of faith.

I think that's what Jesus calls us to do. Adoration is a response to his invitation. And once you make that response, you begin to understand more. It's not understanding like finally getting algebra; it's a different kind of understanding—like loving someone and coming to love and appreciate him or her even more deeply than you already do.

I'm intrigued by your conversion to the Catholic faith. How did your family receive this development?

I have a small family. My parents divorced when I was in the fourth grade. I haven't seen my father since then. I have a seventeen-year-old brother and a fifteen-year-old sister. Plus we're fairly close to my grandmother, but she doesn't live with us.

When my mother found out what I was doing, she was very wary about my conversion. So was my grandmother. In fact, that's an understatement. They became vehemently anti-Catholic; they were totally against my having anything to do with the Catholic faith. First and foremost, they saw the Catholic Church in the same way everyone else does who only knows about it from public opinion, the media and so on. They saw it as sort of a huge business, mind control, superstition-mongers, whatever. [Laughs.] Their instincts were definitely formed by the world, so they were automatically opposed to the Church.

Mainly, though, they saw the Church as completely irrelevant to modern life. And anyone who practices the Catholic faith, or any organized religion actually, was someone to either be suspicious of or feel sorry for. So when they saw me, at such a young age, heading into the Church, they were afraid that I was being influenced or maybe even brainwashed by someone in the Church. So they really were totally against my conversion.

Did they sit you down and have a big talk?

Oh, yeah. We had a lot of arguments. Really loud arguments! We really disagreed fundamentally about the Church.

Did your mom want to lay down the law and just disallow your baptism?

She did do that, at first. She told me that I wasn't going to go through with it. But, at the same time, she respected my intellectual independence, my freedom in matters of the mind. And so she understood that she couldn't forbid me. And there were times when she wanted to speak to my pastor. She just really thought converting was the wrong thing to do and she really wanted to dissuade me from doing it.

Ultimately, there really wasn't anything she could do, and she came to understand. She saw how far into the faith I already was without even being a member of the Church yet.

My conversion also coincided with what I now believe is a call to the priesthood. That's why I'm in seminary. I'm trying to discern whether or not the call is there. But it seems like it is; it seems like God has been calling me to the priesthood all my life, really.

The thing is, I think my mother knew that, too. Although I couldn't explain it. I remember at a young age she would ask me if I was going to be a priest because I was hanging around churches a lot.

You hung around churches when you were a kid? From a reporter's point of view, that's a clear case of "man bites dog"! How did that come about?

My best childhood friend was Catholic. And because I had grown up in a family that was essentially anti-Catholic, I thought his religious views were superstitions. So I didn't think of him as Catholic; I just thought of him as my best friend.

We would go rollerblading or skateboarding, play tennis, whatever. And we would always go to his church's parking lot, just because that's where I wanted to go. It's funny now, because he thought it was a little weird that I always wanted to be near his church. And then we started exploring other churches. If we were downtown, we would go into the cathedral; there was also a small Franciscan chapel downtown and we would sometimes go in there. It became sort of an unspoken thing. We both understood it even though we never really talked about it.

Did you just hang around these churches, or did you go inside?
Oh, we went right in and prayed. But, again, we didn't talk about it. We both kept things to ourselves.

I'm having a hard time picturing two boys going into empty Catholic churches to pray. Toting skateboards, no less.
I don't know. It seemed really natural to us. I think because he was from Poland, raised somewhat strictly Catholic and hadn't known anything else, it didn't seem like an odd thing to him. And meanwhile I had this strong spiritual hunger. His church would always be open. So we'd just go in and hang out, pray and just kind of ... pray!

In front of the tabernacle?
There was an altar rail in this church, and we would go right up to it. And behind the altar rail, the tabernacle was centrally situated, so we were right in front of it. And he taught me how to genuflect—not by talking about it, just by doing it. At first I thought that was kind of weird, but one day I just copied him. Then I always did it, from that day on.

Did he explain to you why you needed to genuflect?

Not really. He just told me God was there. It was a childish answer—
but, then again, we were children.

We would go to various churches. Whenever we were around a
church, we would stop in. And wherever the tabernacle was, he would
always genuflect toward it. I think he understood what he was doing,
and I just kind of imitated him.

Where is your friend now?

Well, we've kind of grown apart. He'll be a junior engineering student
in the fall. He's kind of grown lax in his faith, I'm afraid. I mean, he
fell into the college scene; he's a Christmas and Easter Catholic.

**And yet God, it would seem, used him to introduce you to the
Eucharist.**

I guess you could say that.

**Is your discernment of a vocation something you bring before the
Blessed Sacrament regularly?**

Big time. Now that you mention it, I can't think of a time I haven't
struggled over it in church. I mean, it's always on my mind. Then
again, it's always been on my mind, to one degree or another, as long
as I can remember. I can't remember a time I didn't think I might have
a vocation. I know it sounds funny, but it came naturally—praying
about my vocation and the inclination toward religious life, or priestly
life. It was always inseparable from my conversion. Whenever I had a
hard time about it, I would go to church.

Sometimes, if I felt I really needed to pray about it, I would be there
more than once a day. I came into the seminary this year, at eighteen.

I had been praying about a vocation for a while. And I kind of knew, right at my conversion, that I wanted to go into seminary. I knew that I was being called to discern.

I spend about forty-five minutes a day in silent prayer, and then around an hour for my regular holy hour. And now, during the summer, I go for about an hour to the chapel at my college. They don't have adoration; they just have the tabernacle there. Plus I go to my parish church when they have holy hours.

Where does your mom stand with your discernment now?
Well, I didn't tell her about it until a couple of months before I started college. Like I said, there was something unspoken between us, but she knew I might be going into the priesthood. And that might have been one of the reasons she was so against my conversion.

She was really against my going to seminary, and I never told her about my meetings with the director of vocations for our diocese. She would really have been upset about that. But when the time came in high school to choose a college, she opened my letters for college and she saw that I had checked off theology as my major. And she was upset about that because she knew that usually leads to one of two avenues—teaching or priesthood. Somehow, she knew that.

So it was difficult, but we got around the issue. She didn't want me to go to seminary, and she was very angry at [the vocations director]. She didn't confront him, but I think that was only because I told her not to. But there were quite a few times when she wanted to drive to the office of vocations and have it out with him, or maybe to my parish to let someone know how upset she was about it.

She was angry because she thought they were somehow inducing me to go to seminary, which, if you knew my vocations director, you'd realize couldn't be further from the truth. He's very much about leading you to discernment and letting God take it from there. Yes, he's assertive about encouraging young men to open themselves to the possibility of God's call to the priesthood, but he's very careful to leave the decision to the candidate and God.

I knew this would be a difficult issue with my mom, so I didn't bring it up until a couple of months before the time when I had to submit my application to seminary. And so I eventually did, and she was very disappointed, I think.

By now things have changed for the better. I think that, through me, she's kind of grown in the faith. Or at least she's more knowledgeable about the faith; she's not as ignorant about the Church. I definitely see her converting someday; she's just very stubborn. But she does accept a lot of Church teaching—I would even say all Church teaching. She's just so suspicious of the institutional structure of the Church that she can't yet bring herself to trust the Church.

She's become very supportive of my discernment lately. There's been a complete turnaround. She just wants me to stay true to myself; she doesn't want me to sort of disappear into what she sees as the non-personality of an aloof cleric who doesn't think for himself but just parrots what he's been told to think. [Laughs.]

That's a pretty radical turnaround on your mom's part. What do you think happened to change her mind?
Well, for starters, she's accepted the truth of the Gospel. That's a grace, of course. You can't explain it. But also, we have had so many theological discussions through the years. And she's kind of just opened up little windows here and there along the way. Little windows, each one just enough to let a tiny breeze in. Keep doing that

and pretty soon there's a lot of fresh air coming in.

She comes to church a lot and she's grown less suspicious of the Church. I think she's been accepting Jesus more in her own life, and so she understands the reasons I have for doing what I'm doing. She only wants me to be aware of those reasons; she just wants me to remember why I'm doing this.

How has your time before the Blessed Sacrament helped you to persevere through the adversity you've encountered in your discernment?
I can't imagine going through the discernment process without spending a lot of time before the Blessed Sacrament. I think it's been the only thing that has kept me going sometimes.

For a long time it was like a tug of war between my mother and the Church. It was almost like a propaganda war in my head between the two. You know, she tried to get me off the ecclesial track and the fundamental review of truth that was so critical to me. And sometimes she got through to a certain extent; it seemed like her ideas were against the Church's—not only about what was true but also about what matters. What cut through all that, for me, was the fact that Jesus was always there for me in the Blessed Sacrament. He was like an intermediary. I could go to him whether I converted or not, whether I went to seminary or not. Jesus is still Jesus, and I knew he would still be there in the Blessed Sacrament no matter what I did.

And so the space in front of the tabernacle became kind of like neutral territory I could retreat to when I needed to regroup. You know, you can bring everything in prayer to Jesus in the Eucharist. And that's what I've done. I kind of brought all my anxieties, struggles and what seemed like unresolvable issues before Jesus. And gradually, by God's grace, the answers have been coming.

It's interesting that your mom was not going to be won over to the gospel by intellectual argumentation, no matter how reasoned, logical or well thought out your presentations. But she does have an openness to the love of God, which you experience so intensely in eucharistic devotion.

Yes. She observed my developing love for God, and that made an inroad to her heart. All the intellectual, theological, philosophical and academic tracks of thought that I had been insisting on didn't sway her one bit toward the Gospel. She's very intellectually inclined herself; even though she's not well educated, she can hold her own just fine in those kinds of discussions. And in a lot of ways, her convictions remain the same in those areas. But the love of Jesus, especially in the Blessed Sacrament, so palpable and so far beyond verbal discourse—it's on a higher plane. It's supernatural; it's only really approachable, in the end, by faith. Coming into that is a gradual thing. It's like a gentle drawing of the heart that takes place. The Eucharist changes hearts, not just minds.

Have you encouraged her to pray before the Blessed Sacrament?

She goes to Mass with me sometimes, which would have been unthinkable not that long ago. Sometimes we'll go into churches together outside of Mass, and we'll just take a time-out, I guess you could say. We'll kneel and pray silently together before the tabernacle. She's also been to a couple of Holy Hours.

So she's open to the Eucharist as the real presence of Jesus.

Yes. She understands that, irregardless of the institutional Church, there's Jesus in the Eucharist. And you can do so many things with it. You can process around town, you can have Forty Hours' Devotion, you can have Benediction, you can incense it. But it remains Jesus. Whether it's in an elaborate, expensive monstrance or a little ciborium, it's still the body, blood, soul and divinity of Jesus. And Jesus' love doesn't need all this intellectual substance to support it.

Thinking tries to comprehend reality; it can't create or change reality. I think my mother has come to accept that. Private devotion to the Eucharist allows her to be very devoted to Jesus while avoiding, for the time being, a deep engagement with the institutional Church.

How is your prayer in adoration or before the tabernacle different from other kinds of prayer you do?

I think I've always been somewhat contemplative in my prayer. St. Francis has always been somewhat of a model for me—going into the cave for so many years and then, only after that, coming out and ministering to people and bringing them the Gospel through his actions even more than his words.

A deep prayer life is really the heart of the Christian life. And the Eucharist is the source and summit of the faith itself. So eucharistic adoration provides an outlet and an opportunity for contemplation. What you're doing in making that act of faith, at least for me, is developing a personal relationship with God. And it's squarely on his terms, not your own.

Describe what you mean by contemplative prayer.

For me it's drawing on the grace of God without actively doing anything. It's allowing yourself to be passive, if you will, or docile, silent, before God. When you're before the Blessed Sacrament, and you're open to what the Eucharist is, it's like complete and total self-giving. It's such a great gift from God to give us his physical presence and invite us to just sit for a while with him, that it teaches us to love and to be loved. When you open yourself to the grace of God by responding to that invitation, God opens himself to you. You don't have to do anything. He does it all for you.

Maybe it's the zeal of a convert, but I don't see how you can know what we know as Catholics and not respond to that invitation.

How do you maintain your focus in prayer? Are you ever tempted to daydream?

I don't think I've ever daydreamed, but there are times when you might try to focus yourself by reading Scripture, the Liturgy of the Hours, praying the rosary or using other helps. Those things can pull you back if you're prone to daydreaming—which is natural. All the saints struggled to overcome distractions in prayer, temptations to let their minds wander from God's love.

The main thing is to delve more deeply into the mystery of God's love. Being before the Blessed Sacrament, you're coming to realize, first, that God exists. There is a creator of the universe, and he loves you. For me, just focusing on those two realities allows for very deep contemplation. But that doesn't exclude you from sharing with your Savior all your personal hopes and dreams, along with your problems and struggles.

When you're in this meditative state, before Jesus and with Jesus, you can deal with the issues that are inside of you—the struggles to live the Christian life or to get along with a difficult person in your life. It's kind of a twofold thing, the recognition that God exists and that he loves you with an infinite love. Responding to that, contemplating it and then moving on to whatever you're working on in your life or whatever you're discerning about God's will, God's plan, for your life—in a nutshell, I think that's what eucharistic adoration is all about.

What does deep contemplation in the presence of Jesus feel like?

It's a kind of a fullness of the heart. I don't know that it can be put into words. Sts. Teresa of Avila and John of the Cross probably described it better than anyone else ever did or will. It's the simple realization that God exists and that he loves you with an infinite love. It's simple but infinitely deep.

I've also experienced this at Mass, usually at smaller Masses. You know, a packed Mass at a big parish church gives you a beautiful sense of the presence of God, too, but there's something about the intimacy of Mass and even adoration in a smaller chapel. It may be that there are fewer distractions, and it may be that you have a stronger sense of God's being with you on your own scale.

The feeling is a sense of deep interior peace. You appreciate what the Eucharist is because you begin to understand the sacrifice it took to bring it to you. And you begin to understand the love that's behind the sacrifice. You feel love. And that compels you to love back—to love God and to love other people. So it's really just a peaceful, loving feeling. I can't think of any good way to describe it, so that's really the best I can do on that question.

What would you say to a non-Catholic Christian who is very devoted to Jesus in prayer and the Bible but skeptical about the Blessed Sacrament? An evangelical Protestant, for example.

Well, I'd say of course you can pray to Jesus wherever you are; he is omnipresent, omnisicient and omnipotent. But if you have an understanding of Scripture and a familiarity with the Bread of Life discourse in John 6, and you're familiar with some of the foreshadowings of the Eucharist in the Old Testament, you should look into how it might all be connected. Because it is—the Last Supper, the washing of the feet, the sacrifice on the cross and the resurrection and ascension: They are all connected in this one complete act of self-giving and self-sacrifice.

The Eucharist embodies the totality of God's sacrifice for us. You really can't miss it if you look at the early Church, how much they respected and reverenced the Real Presence, and how the devotion to the Blessed Sacrament developed through the centuries as people became more aware of its significance as the source and summit of Christian life.

I would say just try coming to Mass or even to exposition, and come with an open mind. And keep in mind that God has so radically and completely given himself to us in love that he remains with us in this special, physical way. I don't know what else I could say, but that's what I think I would say.

Are you able to witness the Eucharist to your circle of friends and family?

Well, through my conversion and my entering the seminary, I have a lot of Catholic friends now. My best friend from childhood doesn't really understand my going into the seminary. I have another good friend, a young woman, who's Catholic. I met her in high school, and she was kind of an influence on me. She kind of silently witnessed her faith to me. So we have the faith in common now, and we do share it.

A lot of my friends are Protestants, plus I have some Jewish friends who are not even willing to dialogue. Some of them are curious about why anyone would consider taking a vow of chastity in this day and age, let alone vows of poverty and obedience. But once you explain the faith to them, there's not much they can say. I think they still see the radical commitment as kind of a ridiculous thing to do. I get the sense they'd like to talk me out of it, but what can they do?

What has surprised you most about the life of the Church now that you're not only in it but quite possibly on your way to being a priest?
I think there's a little bit of a crisis in faith lately. There's a loss of that personal intimacy with Jesus. And I think that it's kind of reflective of our world today. There's a lack of inner peace, so that's why there's a lack of external peace among the peoples of the world. People need a place within themselves where they can find a deep interior peace.

The only way that will happen, at least in a way that isn't fundamentally flawed, such as transcendental meditation, which is indifferent to the truth about God and man, is to love and be loved by Jesus. That's what the Eucharist is all about. It's a radical invitation to love and be loved.

CHAPTER 4

Mal

"How many there are who still say, 'I want to see his shape, his image, his clothing, his sandals.' Behold, you do see him, you touch him, you eat him! He gives himself to you not just to be seen, but to be touched, to be eaten, to be received within."

St. John Chrysostom (347–407)

While conducting the interviews for this book, I met Job.

Or what would you call someone who loses his entire family, one member at a time, over a six-year period—and comes away with an even deeper love for God than he had when times were good?

Here's all the background you need to know: Mal, forty-one, a former U.S. Marine, works as a custodian. He converted to the Catholic faith six years ago after a lifetime of practical atheism and considerable debauchery. His scheduled hour for eucharistic adoration is midnight to one each Saturday—"but Jesus is there twenty-four hours a day, seven days a week, so I don't limit myself to my scheduled hour."

Mal's eucharistic adoration witness is tightly intertwined with the story of his life, as you'll see. I wish I had the space to run every word of our long conversation, because it was all astonishing, but I've had to make substantial cuts to make sure I fit in the most important parts. This is one memorable testimony to God's grace.

A mutual friend of ours told me bits and pieces of your story. I'm eager to hear the whole thing.

Well, my conversion came through suffering. And I've realized that people don't understand how God's love can come to us, if we let it, through suffering. The Catholic Church has always taught this, very deeply and beautifully, but sometimes we aren't ready to listen until we've actually done some suffering.

I guess it all started when my stepson was murdered. That was back in 1993. I had been in the Marine Corps and hadn't lived the most godly life. I'm a recovering alcoholic, and the anger that I felt when he was murdered—let's put it this way: I actually thought of ways to murder the kid who did it. I used to lie in bed at night, unable to sleep because I was just so filled with thoughts of hate and vengeance.

How did the murder happen?

It was strange because it happened a few months after I got into a terrible car accident, which was the result of my drinking. My wife, Cathy, had told me while I was lying in my hospital bed, with no memory of how I had gotten there, that if I didn't give up drinking and change my ways, then that would be it for our marriage. She was the only person I had ever loved enough to sacrifice anything for, and I could see that she was serious. So that was it. I gave it all up, cold turkey, right then and there.

About four months later, Justin, who was then eighteen, was at a pool hall. He got into some kind of scrape with a kid who was from out of town. This other kid was from a big city hours away. I have no idea what brought him to our little town. Whatever the dispute was, this kid stabbed my stepson to death. He stabbed my boy in the heart.

Now, you have to realize that, when I fell in love with my wife, I fell in love with her two kids, too. Because of my promiscuity in my younger days, especially in the Marines, I could not get my wife pregnant. Yet God had given me these two beautiful stepchildren when he gave me my beautiful wife.

Even though at the time I had no faith in God at all, I was thinking of God the night of Justin's murder. It's really strange, thinking back. I was coming home late, after working second shift, and I was thinking about how good God had been to me, to give me a wonderful wife and two beautiful children even though I couldn't have children of my own. And so I pulled into the driveway with that exact thought running through my head.

Right away I knew something was wrong because there were no cars in the driveway. When I walked in the house, my in-laws were there. They said, "Get to the hospital immediately." Well, the minute I walked into the hospital, I heard the most blood-curdling scream I've ever heard in my life. It was Cathy. They had just pronounced Justin dead.

The whole thing was incredible. I look back on it now and I can see where God was saying to me, "You have got some serious stuff coming down the road. And your wife doesn't need another child to take care of. She needs a man. A real man, a sober man. Someone who can help her with what she's going to go through."

So it was as if God had used my accident to sober me up and prepare me for this moment, which itself would turn out to be more preparation for even more suffering to come for my wife and for me.

Along with grief, you were filled with rage.
I was filled with hate. I was angry enough to kill. Because here I was, the big, tough marine. Nothing could touch me; I take care of everything. I take care of my family, my friends, everything. And now all of

a sudden I'm looking at my wife and she's just a complete mess and I want to fix it but I can't do a single thing about it. I can't do anything to bring Justin back and make everything OK for her again.

They wound up catching the kid who did it, and he did prison time. He was only sixteen at the time of the murder. But still, I was just filled with rage at this kid. Not only for robbing Justin of his life, but for what he had done to the whole fabric of our family. We immediately started coming apart at the seams.

Cathy was just a total mess. Justin's death came at a particularly bad time for her because her mother was dying of a terminal disease. And, after Justin's death, both of us became super-protective—overprotective, really—of Jill. We were so scared of anything happening to her.

Well, a year goes by and Jill, who's now sixteen, starts feeling lousy. We take her in and she's diagnosed with non-Hodgkins lymphoma. And this was just unbearable. It was too much, coming just a year after we lose our son and we're still recovering from that. We couldn't believe it. We asked ourselves, "Why is God doing this to us?"

Jill was a beautiful girl. I mean, genuinely. A cheerleader, very smart, the kind of kid who would cheer everyone up. The irony of her getting this disease was that she wanted to become a pediatric oncologist.

And it was really with her that the conversions started for us. She had gone to Franciscan University of Steubenville for a conference, at the invitation of the pastor with the youth group at her parish. See, she was the only one going to Sunday Mass. She went with her grandmother, and they never missed.

Before that trip, she had been the typical teenage girl. Always in front of the mirror, always worried about how she looked. She came back from that conference and I remember saying to my wife, "Cathy, there's something different about Jill." She said, "What?" I said, "I don't know. Something good."

Gradually, the change in Jill had an effect on my wife and me. One of the things that struck me, looking back, was the incredible love Jill and Cathy had for one another. It was a love that could not be contained. It spread to me. I think God showed me that so I could understand the Trinity a little better—how the Holy Spirit is the love that flows between the Father and the Son. I didn't know that at the time, but I remember looking back at it later and having that realization. When I came to the faith, it was the first thing I thought of. I said, "That love was so powerful, it couldn't be contained." It spread to anyone who was around it. And I was around it a lot.

In fact, the conversions that ended up taking place in our area—our extended family, our neighborhood, our parish community—all because of Jill were remarkable.

Jill and Cathy would be reading the Bible at night together, lying in bed. I used to tease them. I'd say, "Would you please cut the umbilical cord?" Because they were constantly sitting close to each other, just being together so close. When Jill was in the hospital, Cathy never left her side. She quit her job so she could be there with Jill through it all. I think there may have been one hour when Cathy had to do something; except for that, she was there with Jill every second of every day.

Jill was keeping a diary as she went through this, and some of the things she wrote were saintly. I mean, really, really saintly. She wrote, "I used to be the most vain person in the world. I used to sit in front of the mirror, looking at my hair, my clothes, my makeup, and think about how attractive I could be to the world, how much the boys would like me. Now I look in the mirror and I see a girl with no hair, with eyes bulging out of her head, with teeth yellowed from chemotherapy. And yet I see more beauty than I ever did when I was beautiful by the world's standards. Why? Because Jesus Christ loves me."

Well, that just blew me right out of the water. I thought, where is she finding this? I just can't fathom it.

I also remember saying to someone at work, "If anything happens to Jill, my wife will commit suicide. Because she's just so close to her, they're attached at the hip like Siamese twins."

Well, a year after the diagnosis, Jill died. It had only been two years since we lost Justin. I thought Cathy was going to be a suicide case at that point, but it was just the opposite. Jill had been witnessing Christ to her mother all the time she was dying. It was another case of God blowing my mind, showing me something in the people around me that I didn't know existed for real anywhere. A couple of months after Jill died, I said to a coworker, "Cathy and I are going to get divorced." She said, "What are you talking about?" I said, "She found a better man. She found Jesus, and I can't compete."

Cathy wasn't pushing me away. It's just that, as her faith was really deepening, and her personal relationship with Jesus was taking off, I couldn't fathom what was happening. She was spending a lot of time out of the house, going to Mass, youth group, all sorts of church-related activities. It didn't bother me, because I figured that's what she needed to do to survive this incredible pain. I just didn't think we were going to make it.

Right about now you've got to be questioning your own life, and the meaning of life, yourself.

Well, Cathy's mother had frequently said to me, "You need to get baptized." I would say, "Oh, that's a bunch of bull. If there's a God, I'm sure he loves me whether or not I have water sprinkled over my head." I had no understanding whatsoever about any of the sacraments. It seemed like a hodgepodge; it didn't make sense to me. If there is a God, and he created us and loves us, why do we have to go through these religious rituals?

For my wife's sake, I started attending the RCIA program at her parish. She had said, "I cannot go through life without receiving Jesus [in Communion]. And in order for me to do that, either you have to leave or we have to have our marriage blessed by the Church." She immediately started pursuing an annulment for her first marriage.

And I'm thinking, "I don't understand this Catholic Church; this stuff seems whacked out. They make these rules, and all they want is your money." So I went through the motions and said, "Yeah, right, I'll go through RCIA."

Well, one night Cathy says to me, "Mal, some friends of mine from Church are having some people over. I'd really like it if you'd come." I was coming around to God a little bit, but the faith still really wasn't there. And these people were, to me, religious fanatics. So I said, "Please, Cathy, don't make me! I'm not like those people." Well, she knew just what to say to that. She said, "Mal, you always say you don't have a prejudiced bone in your body. And yet you don't like religious people."

And she was right. She had me. I said, "OK, you win. I'll go with you." And she said, "And you'll go with an open heart." And, for some reason, I even agreed to that.

So we were there about an hour, and I'm saying to myself, "Well, they're nice enough people. They don't have cliques; they all respect each other and get along. Nice people." Pretty soon the host family's son, who was discerning a call to the priesthood at the time, walks through the door. And right behind him is this guy with a beard in a gray robe. He was a Franciscan friar, though I didn't know it at the time.

Somehow I started talking to this man, and he looked at me and it was as if his eyes pierced my soul. I mean, I looked him in the eye and he looked, with love, right into my soul. That was how it felt. Later I prayed, "God, I don't know what that man has, but whatever it is, I want it!"

Eventually, I found out what that man had. It was a long process, but I found out. He had Jesus. By now I know this man well. He's an incredible priest, a beautiful human being. He's spent a lot of time in prison for pro-life activities. He was, and may still be, the most *in persona Christi* priest I've ever met. It was just obvious to me at that moment that I had a gnawing emptiness; I was aware of it because it was just as obvious that this man was full to the brim with the theological virtues—faith, hope and love.

Anyway, to make a long story short, I finally came to know Jesus Christ. I fell so in love with Jesus, I didn't know what to do with myself. And it all started with the simple witness of that friar's life at this little get-together I didn't even want to go to. This man had nothing that the world told me would make me happy. He didn't have sex, he didn't have money and he dressed like an idiot. He had taken vows of poverty, chastity and obedience. And yet he was happy with a deep happiness I couldn't even comprehend. His joy was so real, so palpable. And I was miserable even though I was surrounded by things, by all the things I had spent my life chasing after.

You can't fake what that friar has. If it was fake, believe me, I could have spotted it a mile away. I was very in the world and an ex-marine; I had a very finely tuned hot-air detector. The only way to describe it is, I felt filthy in his presence. Because I knew I was in the presence of holiness. It was very humbling and the most eye-opening experience of my entire life.

So Justin is dead two years, Jill is dead six months, Cathy is becoming very religious and here you are having the beginnings of a real conversion experience yourself.

It's a miracle, really, all the little things God did to "propose" to me, for lack of a better word. I've tried, and I can't explain it to myself any other way. I didn't enter into this; I didn't want it. I was reasonably happy where I was. I didn't think I needed more God in my life. But God put himself in front of me, I now realize, out of such love and mercy that I can't even fathom it. He loved me so much, and he wanted me to know his love, his peace.

Which brings me to eucharistic adoration, why it's so important to me.

First you have to tell me about your wife, what happened there.

Oh, my wife was top-notch. She was the best lady I've ever met in my life—my best friend, ever. Ultimately we each helped the other draw closer to Christ, which is the point of a Christian marriage.

We were on vacation in 1998, three years after Jillian died. We were in Costa Rica, we and another couple, and we were driving out to see the rain forest. I was driving. We were coming down this hill, going very slowly. Maybe two miles an hour. It had rained, so the dirt road was muddy. And there was a little bridge at the bottom of this steep hill. It was only one lane, even though it was meant for two cars. So I'm looking to make sure no cars are coming from the other direction. As I tapped the brake to edge forward, the wheels started sliding. And they kept sliding and sliding. Very slowly.

So we slid onto this narrow little bridge on this steep hill, and there was no guardrail on either side. It was a forty-foot drop off the side. And the front right tire slipped off the edge. So we were teetering there, rocking. Cathy was in the backseat on the passenger side. My friend was sitting next to me in front, and his wife was in the back behind me. I prayed, "Please, God, let us tilt to the left."

Just as I said the word "left," we fell over, to the right. The last words I heard my wife say were, "Oh, my God." It wasn't a frenzied, panicky voice. It was a beautiful, soft, almost peaceful voice. The Jeep fell forty feet and landed right on the roof. It didn't roll; it just sort of hit and stuck, upside-down.

I was pinned—my foot was stuck somehow—and there was water coming in. I thought I was going to drown. I'm thinking, "I've got to get to Cathy." I'm struggling as hard as I can to get myself free. I've got blood running down my face from a cut on my head; it's running into my eyes and my mouth. And all of a sudden, inexplicably, I stopped struggling. I knew she was gone. I don't know how I knew; I just knew. We two had really become one, and now there was just an emptiness there. I knew her soul had departed before I ever even got to her. Finally my foot popped out of my sneaker and I crawled out.

Apart from Cathy being the only one to die in that accident—it seemed like a miracle that the other three of us walked away with only minor injuries—the thing that was really amazing was, these friends of ours were Jewish. And yet Rich said to me later, "Mal, I felt the presence of Jesus Christ in that Jeep when Cathy died." I said, "But, Rich, you don't believe in Jesus." He said, "I know. I can't explain it myself."

So, looking back at losing my wife, on top of losing my two stepchildren whom I loved with all my heart, just like my own children, I can see how God was preparing me for the day when I would really need him. I had no way of knowing what that day would look like. But it came. And I was ready for it when it did. Just by being in Christ, by being so deeply grateful to him for forgiving me for the horrible life I had lived and so in love with him just for being there.

You were already "in Christ" when the accident happened?
I was very close to the Lord when I lost my wife. But losing Cathy, somehow, took me to an even higher level of love for Jesus.

How so?
I have no idea. It makes no sense. I loved my wife so much. And I miss her so much, to this day. And yet I'm sitting here talking to you, just like I talk to everyone, about Jesus. He's all I want to talk about anymore. I can't believe how much I love him. Me, an old, tough-guy marine with a sordid past of total sin and depravity. I love Jesus with all my heart, all my soul and all my strength. Believe me, I don't understand God any more than anyone else. I just know I love him.

You must have gone through a period of intense grief, though. Did you not?
I went through a period of very intense grief. I walked around for about three months running on nothing but God's grace. He just carried me because I couldn't carry myself. And then it all hit, what had happened to me. The sense of loss was just overwhelming. I can't describe what it was like; it was just ... *hard.*

And yet not one minute did I suffer alone. He was always with me. Jesus was always with me.

I've had one dream about my wife. Only one. I don't put any stock in it as a vision or anything like that, but I'll tell you about it because it involves adoration. I had it on my birthday, almost a year after losing her. I left work early because I felt ill. My head was pounding. I went home and lay down and I was out like a light in minutes. About an hour later the phone rings, wakes me from a sound sleep. I get up, feeling just miserable. I answer the phone, and it's my sister calling from Florida to wish me a happy birthday. If not for that call, I probably wouldn't have remembered the dream so vividly. So I like to think it was the Blessed Mother who moved my sister to call me at that moment!

In my dream, Cathy was coming out of the adoration chapel. I looked at her and she was absolutely radiant. She was wearing clothes she normally wore. I said, "Cathy!" And she ignored me. I called her again. "Cath!" She walked out the door, toward the parking lot. And everything was exactly as it is in our adoration chapel. It wasn't dreamlike, where things are strange and mixed up. Everything was normal— except that my deceased wife was there. She turned around and looked at me and said, with great love and compassion, "*I hear you every single day.*" And that was it. The phone rang and I woke up.

Like I say, I don't put a lot of stock in dreams. God can reach us that way; he reached a number of people in Scripture like that, but it's dangerous to assume that any particular dream is sent by God. But I do hold out a part of me that hopes God was behind that particular dream.

Either way, it built me up. Whether it was God or my subconscious psyche, it was a reminder of the Christian hope that we have in Christ: One day we will be reunited—all of us, not couples per se because we know there is no marriage in heaven, but all of us in Christ.

Now back up a bit and tell me about how you got involved with eucharistic adoration.

Oh, that's the kicker. I went to confession; my confessor was the Franciscan priest whose witness had moved me so much at the party. I was still young in the faith, still being fed milk, as they say. So my confession that first time was very superficial. Get in, get out. I wasn't recollected or anything, and I'm sure that came through. In any case, for my penance, he gave me an hour of eucharistic adoration every week for several weeks.

Needless to say, as the weeks went by, my confessions got a lot more sincere. My life got a lot more sincere. And a lot better. In fact, gradually, everything got a lot better. When you go before the Lord of the universe—failed, humbled, on your knees—there's no way to explain what happens. I can't find the words for you because I really don't understand it myself. I just go in there and tell him how much I love him. Tell him how useless I am without him. Tell him that I have no virtue, that there is nothing good in me, that I have nothing to offer or give. But I am open to receiving whatever goodness he wants to give me. And he always gives it to me.

What does he give you?

Everything. Peace. Love. Himself. That's what he gives me. Jesus gives me himself. See, that's the thing about adoration: It's really preparation to receive Jesus in Communion. You adore him and then you get to receive him, and when you do, it's like, does it get any better than this? He transforms me into what I'm not, what I could never make of myself. He makes me into himself, a part of himself. I don't know what else to tell you about it. Nothing else can come close to receiving Jesus—body and blood, soul and divinity. Nothing.

So this was the beginning of your really "giving God permission," as Mother Teresa used to say, to be first in your life.

Yes. Until that penance, I hadn't really experienced adoration as a personal, one-on-one visit with Jesus. I had been to a Youth 2000 event where they had overnight exposition, and lots of people were there praying before Jesus all through the night, but I had never been alone with him in that way until that penance. I had never gone and talked to Jesus like I do in adoration. I mean, I loved him and he had done wonderful things in my life, but I wasn't really in relationship with him. It was through adoration that I got into this deep—you'd have to call it intimate—relationship.

After I got a taste of adoration by doing penance, I wanted to go back again and again. What started out as penance, something I had to do to atone for my sins, became something very sweet, something I wanted to do out of love. Something, in fact, I couldn't get enough of. So that was when I signed up for an hour every week at a parish across town that has perpetual adoration.

How long did that phase of the relationship last? Others have told me the "honeymoon phase" doesn't last any more than it does in a marriage.

That's definitely true. See, God takes us right where we're at. And when I started with those first few adoration hours in penance, he gave me some spiritual candy, so to speak. Those good feelings, that warm glow of just being there with him so close. The problem was, of course, that I was more concerned with pursuing a feeling than performing an act of faith—which, of course, is far more meritorious in God's sight if you *don't* have consolations and good feelings. Love, like the other theological virtues, faith and hope, is first an act of the will. If you're loving someone only because you're getting something from that person, then you aren't really loving him or her.

That was around six years ago, when you still had Jillian and Cathy. What is adoration like for you now?

These days, I just sometimes kneel there in awe. To be there in the presence of Christ—the same Christ who walked on water, who stopped the woman's hemorrhage when she grabbed his cloak, the same Christ who did all those things in the Gospels. He is now right in front of my eyes, alone with me here. What an unbelievable privilege to be in there with him. It's just mind-boggling. You could sit there forever because the peace that radiates from the Lord—you just know that that's truly "my Lord and my God," as St. Thomas said.

I mean, I don't bring anything. I go through my acts of adoration, contrition, supplication and thanksgiving. And I go through my usual routines, but it's really just the presence of Jesus that blows me away. I can tell God anything. I can just sit there and know that this person absolutely delights in me, exactly as I am. That the only thing he wants from me is my sin. It's the only thing about me that he doesn't own.

I sometimes find myself thinking of my relationship with Jesus in terms of the relationship I knew with my wife. You have to desire giving more than getting. If you go into any relationship only looking for what you can get, you've got a dead relationship on your hands. In the same way, if you were to approach Jesus like a cosmic moneybags—you give him your prayer and devotion only as long as he pays you or rewards you for it—you would not be in relationship with Jesus very long. Because the goodies are going to dry up; he's going to let that happen so you can really learn to love him. No, I love Jesus because he is truth.

And that's the key thing I really found out through eucharistic adoration: He is exactly who he said he is. The way I am, a certain part of me approached Jesus saying, "If I can catch him in a lie, I don't have to believe." Well, it's been six years and I still haven't caught him in a lie. And believe me, it's not as if, on some subconscious level, I haven't been trying.

Eventually, a certain dryness started to seep into your prayer life, including in adoration?

So much dryness. I mean, there have been a lot of times when I felt as if I was going through the motions, but for nothing. In fact, the sweetness really only lasted about three months. It was three months of candy where I was constantly getting consolations, interior reinforcements and encouragements. That period was too short, but that's the way it went for me.

The thing is, when the dryness started, I stayed honest with Jesus. I'd say, "Lord, I bring nothing to the table. I don't even want to be here tonight. I'm tired, I'm miserable. I don't even want to be with you." And he even accepted that! That was the thing that always amazed me. He accepted whatever I brought, no matter how halfheartedly I offered it.

Here's the God of the universe, and I know it's him, and I can be that open and honest with him. Why? Because he knows me better than I know myself. And as I look back, I realize that was when the real relationship began. It was no longer a child coming around for candy. There was a real depth developing as I came in and prayed, "No matter what, Lord, just to be in your presence—even if I can't bring anything and I feel I'm not receiving anything, at least I'm with you."

Sometimes I would read from Scripture or the lives of the saints. Just hungry to get to know Jesus better today than I knew him yesterday.

What difference does eucharistic adoration make in your life?

If Jesus didn't make himself available for me to be close to in this way, I think my faith would be much more superficial. He challenges me when I go in there. You can't very well sit in Jesus' presence hour after hour, week after week, and tell him how much you love him, how much you want to follow him and be close to him and change for him—and then go and casually commit all kinds of little sins. You go and do what you told him you would do.

He might be telling me, "You need to work on your anger." Or this needs to be worked on or that needs to be worked on. And I see his tremendous humility and love, coming to me in such a humble way— under the appearance of plain, man-made bread—and know that he is calling me to the same kind of humility and love. And that's most especially what I've gotten through eucharistic adoration: humility.

As a side benefit, I've also gotten a sense of spiritual progress. It's been slow but sure.

When opportunities present themselves for you to go and witness the Gospel, do you take them more than you did before you discovered adoration?

Absolutely. When I went to work at my old job, at a very wealthy high-tech company where I was just as caught up as anyone else striving to get ahead, I used to get this all the time when my conversion first started taking hold: "Who are you trying to impress?" People didn't buy it. Gradually, though, as you accept what God has chosen to give you, your whole attitude changes. And that changes other people's attitudes toward you.

The bottom line that comes screaming through, so gentle yet so firm, as I walk out of adoration is: Live it. Don't preach it or argue it.

Just live it. That's what St. Francis told the brothers: "Go and tell the world about Jesus; only use words if you have to." And the greatest part about living the Gospel is that it's OK to fail. In fact, it's good to fail because it increases your humility and your reliance on God.

Before my conversion, I was ambitious in the worldly way, like everyone around me was. I loved things and used people. Now I love people and use things. Everything can be replaced except for people. Individual humans are the rarest and most valuable things of all, the only really valuable things, on the face of the earth. It's amazing the peace you can bring to others when you look at them and remain mindful of that truth.

This is why we love the sinner but hate the sin—because of what sin does to that rare gem of God, that individual human soul.

I have a brother who is a homosexual. And I tell him: "I love you too much not to tell you that what you're doing has eternal consequences." And I also said that to a couple of homosexuals who worked for the same company as I did when I was in the secular world. Naturally, the response you get, at least initially, is not one of receptivity.

But you can't sell out the Gospel to be nice or well-liked. Love isn't about being nice; it's about genuinely caring for the state of others' souls. You can "nice" people all the way to hell by failing to tell them about Jesus and the forgiveness he offers for whatever sin they're living in.

I wouldn't have the inclination, let alone the guts, to even say anything to people stuck in that lifestyle or any sinful situation. But every week I go in front of whom I want to be like. And Jesus never, ever shied from calling sin what it was just not to ruffle someone's feathers. In fact, he seemed to have greater compassion for the sinners than the righteous. He called them out of their sin because he loved them too much to watch them die in their sin. Should those of us who want to be his disciples be doing something different?

What makes you so sure you're in the actual, physical presence of Jesus when you're before the Blessed Sacrament?

The effect it has on me. I am becoming more like him whom I am adoring. If that's not Jesus under the appearance of bread, as my faith and two thousand years of Church teaching tell me, then why am I being transformed so radically? Is a piece of bread making me into something I'm not? If I go into a garage and meditate on the car, am I going to develop wheels and a chassis?

If that's not Jesus Christ up there, I can't explain how or why a person who was filled with selfish longing, anger, hate, rage, jealousy, envy—you name a vice, I had it in spades—is becoming the person you're talking to. Someone who doesn't have a whole lot of interest in talking about anything but Jesus. Someone who now knows what love and peace and tranquility are. If these changes could have come about by looking at the wall, I guess I'd sit and stare at the wall. My eyes are opened; my heart is new.

You'll have to trust me when I tell you, because you didn't know me before: What you see in me is radical transformation. And it's Jesus' doing, not mine.

I think what amazes me most about your devotion is that you don't look back at your terrible sufferings or your long list of sins. Nor are you terribly concerned about what tomorrow might bring, about earning a lot of money or that sort of thing. You're clearly oriented on the present moment.

Well, I think that's one of the best things about walking with Jesus. All we have is right now. Yesterday is gone and tomorrow may never come.

I will never wallow in self-pity over the sufferings I have been through. If you want to have self-pity, go look at a crucifix. Then try to pity yourself. If you can pity yourself after looking at Jesus hanging on that cross, you're even more self-indulgent than I ever was; we need to get you some serious help. I don't know how anyone who's aware of what Jesus suffered for us could pity himself. I can't do it, and I've lost the three people I've been closest to in my whole life. But look at Jesus up on that cross—for us selfish sinners. That's suffering. That's love.

To me, that image is such a stark, hard reality. It's not just a statue or a painting by some great Renaissance master. That's God up on that cross. It's not some fictional character thought up by an ancient story-teller. And Jesus could have stopped the whole thing at any time. I didn't have that choice—I couldn't have stopped my sufferings if I wanted to. But I had Jesus up there on the cross to suffer with me. And that made it not only tolerable but, more importantly, meaningful.

Archbishop Fulton Sheen used to say that there's a lot of wasted suffering, meaning that modern people don't see the opportunity to suffer as the tremendous grace the Church has always said it is. Every trial, every pain, is a chance to unite our suffering with Jesus', a means of building up the entire body of Christ, as St. Paul spelled out.

This is not to say that I look down on people who need to talk about their suffering, and some people need to talk about it a lot. I remember someone saying to me, "How can you sit there and listen to that woman complaining about all her little headaches?" I said, "Because her headaches are real. They are her cross. God didn't give her a big cross; he gave her one that he knew she'd be able to carry." It's not for me to judge. For one person, a hangnail might seem like too much to bear. That might be all the cross that person can carry. But God gave me this cross, the cross of losing the people I loved, for whatever reason. He knows what cross I need to get me into heaven, to be by his side, for all eternity. And I'll gladly carry it for his glory.

Most of your life is oriented around the Church now.
True. I play a little golf. Maybe a little too much, sometimes! But it's true that I don't have a lot of outside interests. I am a very happy person and I don't knock people who fill their lives with what now seem to me like trivial pursuits. But when you have the best—when you're in love with the best—why would you want to spend a lot of time away from him?

I have found what makes me extremely joyful. Not so much happy but joyful. I teach CCD, and one of the things the kids always ask me when they see my passion for God is, "Don't you ever go out and party and have a good time?" I don't want to get caught up in telling them about just how much I used to party, or even all the good things I used to be very active in—sports and so on—so I just tell them: I used to be very competitive. I was into a lot of things the world encourages you to get into. And I really enjoyed them a lot. But now I'm in the greatest competition ever. And I'm having the most fun I've ever had. The competition is with myself—to be more holy, more Christlike today than I was yesterday. And don't ask me why, but this competition is a blast. And you know what? I'm not exaggerating one bit.

I also tell them that they're receiving a lot of enticements from the world to explore this path and that, an endless string of suggestions that true happiness lies in using people and loving things. But if they'll also keep a channel open to hear God's voice along with all those voices on the TV, in the movies, in their music and magazines and all, then, when they do find the pearl of great price, they'll sell all that other stuff to get it. And the pearl, of course, will be Jesus.

How would you witness about eucharistic adoration to a luke-warm Catholic who feels he or she doesn't have the time?
You hit the nail on the head when you talk about time. People are very protective of their time. They look at an hour a week commitment to something like adoration and all they can think is, I don't know if I can give that hour up every week. They look at their time as the most precious thing they have—and, of course, they're right.

The thing is, you will never outdo God in generosity. Your time in adoration will never be wasted, and you'll never give up more than you get. If they only understood what you get through eucharistic adoration, they'd want to be in adoration one hundred hours a week.

You just get so much in return for that one hour you give to God in this special way. You go in, you give him an hour—and he takes care of your life. He fills in all the holes and gets you started building eternal mansions in heaven. Not a bad deal if you ask me.

If I could say one thing to anybody who's going to read this, it would be: "Love is sitting there, waiting for you." He is absolute love, and that's what you can become. By sitting in the presence of love, you will want to become love. And you will receive the graces to actually allow that to happen to yourself.

What a beautiful world we would live in if people only knew.

CHAPTER 5

Paula

"He took earth from earth, because flesh is from the earth, and he took Flesh of the flesh of Mary. He walked on earth in that same Flesh, and gave that same Flesh to us to be eaten for our salvation. Moreover no one eats that Flesh unless he has adored it ... and we sin by not adoring it."

St. Augustine (354–430)

I look at my notes from my conversation with Paula, and I hardly know where to begin in introducing her.

Like Mal, she lived through a series of tragedies and disasters that seem lifted from the pages of a novel. Yet, also like Mal, she turned to God in the hour of her deepest need—and found herself led, inexorably, if only gradually, to a profound devotion to Jesus Christ in the Blessed Sacrament.

But it wasn't just the substance of her story that I found so moving. It was also her evident courage, candor and genuineness, revealed in unguarded mannerisms and a hushed tone of voice, in talking about her decidedly troubled past.

Initially Paula balked at my request for an interview. She admitted she was nervous and expressed doubt that she had anything to say that others might learn from. When I first turned on my tape recorder—on a visit to the home she shares with her husband, two children and one friendly spaniel, all of whom were playing outside as we spoke—she visibly tensed up. I thought she was going to call the whole thing off. But as soon as she got rolling on my first question, she seemed to forget the recorder was there: Out came a two-hour rush of words that, by turns, had my mouth gaping with shock, my chest heaving with relief, my sides rocking with laughter and my throat fending off a lump.

And that was before she even got to the part about eucharistic adoration.

Her incredible testimony, in fewer than five hundred words:

Paula grew up the middle of three girls in a nominally Catholic family. Church was something other people did. "You can tell when your parents really don't believe," she says. "As far as I was concerned, Jesus went out with Santa Claus and the Easter Bunny."

Her parents never got along; they divorced when she was a teenager. While her sisters went on to find success and achievement on the straight and narrow, she decided she was the black sheep—and headed straight for the ditch.

"I was always unhappy and insecure, anxious and afraid," she told me. "I felt like I always had to have a boyfriend to make me feel like I was worth anything. All through my teens and a lot of my twenties, I went from one boyfriend to the next in search of self-worth and security."

One day, she was riding on the back of a boyfriend's motorcycle when a car slammed into them from the side. He walked away; she was nearly killed and her leg almost severed. She went through multiple grafts, joint reconstructions and other major surgeries to save it, and was in a full leg cast for a year. While recuperating, and against the advice of family and friends, she married the man. Soon after, his behavior turned bizarre and abusive. Paula escaped with her belongings from their second-floor apartment while he was out, no small accomplishment with a severely injured leg. (She eventually divorced the man and had the marriage annulled by the Church.)

One night not long after, she was getting out of her car on the outskirts of the inner city—there to visit another boyfriend—when a stranger jumped her from behind, put a knife to her throat and dragged her into the dark of a field. He tied her up and raped her for an hour. He untied her when she promised to try to help him with his problems, which he had angrily recounted throughout the attack, then ran off when Paula's boyfriend came looking for her, calling her name.

Paula eventually reached the point where suicide seemed the only solution to her life, which she says seemed like "one long, downward spiral" into a dark abyss. But God had other plans: The day she planned to overdose, an old friend she'd not heard from in years called to invite her to a Protestant pentecostal prayer service. The friend, it turned out, had undergone a profound conversion to Christ and was looking up old friends to witness to. The friend's words were the first glint of light she'd seen since she could recall.

So began, under circumstances she sees as "so obviously set up by God to save me from myself," her own radical conversion to Christ.

The details of Paula's testimony are too involved to recount adequately here. Suffice it to say that she finally found her way home to the Catholic Church, and—with her home, family and God now at the center of her life for going on twenty years—has "everything I ever wanted, though I didn't know what I wanted until I fell in love with Jesus."

Wow. That's quite a testimony—and we haven't even gotten to the real presence of Jesus in the Eucharist yet.

I believed the Real Presence to be true after I fell in love with Jesus through prayer, spiritual readings and the Mass. As far as experiencing him in adoration, and knowing for a fact that it is he under the appearance of bread and wine, I had already been transformed in my love for him through the Mass. I mean, I would go up to Communion in a completely normal state of mind. And then I would receive Jesus and would be—I can't even describe it as crying. It was crying, but it wasn't out of pain or sadness or even the intense kind of happiness that sometimes makes you cry, like when a close friend has a baby. It was a joy so deep that I really can't even describe it in words. Joy that Jesus is real, and joy about his presence with me and in me.

Today, I rarely feel that anymore. But for a long time I did, and it was unbelievable. I couldn't wait to get to Mass, and I mean every day. And then a friend of mine at the parish said to me one day, "You know, they have adoration every weekday after Mass, until 9 o'clock." And I hadn't even been in the adoration chapel yet. One of the reasons was that the confessionals were in there and, even then, I was still avoiding the Sacrament of Reconciliation, crazy as that seems to me now.

God moved my friend to very gently say to me, "You know, Paula, you would really like adoration." She described the room; she said there were comfortable seats and that you didn't need to kneel the whole time or stay for a whole hour, that there were people in and out all the time. So that gave me the courage to go in. I was still the kind of person who was always afraid, and at that point, I was afraid of not knowing what to do, how to act, in a little chapel like that. I didn't know what was in there—I had never even so much as peeked in the door.

So I went, and after that first time going, I wanted to go back every day. And I very nearly did just that. Just when I needed God the most, he cleared a lot of things out of the way and made it possible for me to make him the central part of my life.

It used to be wonderful to be alone with Jesus in the adoration chapel. Back then, I had him all to myself a lot of the time. Now that adoration has become so popular, it's very rare that you're not sharing him with other people. In the past year, I've been alone with Jesus in the chapel I think only twice.

How does having lots of company in the chapel affect your experience of Jesus in adoration?

You know, I don't know if it was better before because it was the "honeymoon" period when I was still falling in love with Jesus, or if it was better because I was alone with him so much of the time. He was really just pouring such graces out on me during that period of my life that it's hard to tell what in me made me especially open to receiving them. To be really honest, it's not like that for me anymore. I'm going through a rather dry period. I've been in it for about a year. Sometimes in adoration, I look and look and I just can't imagine that he's there. I believe in my mind that he is, and I do everything I was doing before. As far as my prayers and everything are concerned, it's just not as easy. It's not coming to me as naturally as it once did.

I remember what an adventure it used to be to pray the rosary. Every mystery just came alive. Now I announce the mystery, I think about it for a moment and then I go through the prayers. Before I used to talk to Jesus about where he was in the mystery, and I felt as if I was there with him. I mean, I would go through the most beautiful experiences with him. Lately it's not like that. It's gotten very hard.

But, you know, I beat myself up for a long time about this. I thought it was because of laxity that I had gotten to this point. Now I don't think that's really it, because I'm still looking for him very hard. But I actually used to see him, with my heart. When I was praying, and he did reveal himself, I was looking very hard for him.

What was that like? How was it that you "saw" Jesus?

The only way I can describe what I felt like at those high points in my relationship with Jesus is that I kind of caught him looking at me, with great love, if you can try to imagine what I mean by that. And the reason I know it wasn't just a figment of my imagination is that, when I'm praying, I close my eyes. And I don't know what it's like for anyone else—this is such a personal thing—but I would be looking hard for Jesus, with my eyes gently closed, while I was praying. And while I'd be looking for him on one side, he'd be over on the other. I know that doesn't explain anything, but that's the best way I can explain something I really have no words for. It's too beautiful to put into words. I'm sorry I can't do better than that.

You're doing fine. What was it like when you first started to experience the real presence of Christ in eucharistic adoration?

It's so much easier to talk about the miraculous and earth-shattering things; it's much harder to describe the more subtle things that happen in adoration. It would be like trying to describe the love and the security you have, and somewhat take for granted, in your family and closest friends. You could tell people what you do for and with one another, and you'd tend to talk about the big things—birthday parties, Christmas presents, vacations together, whatever—but the relationship, the bond itself, isn't moving from one big thing to the next. It's really in countless little moments. It's in the trust, sensitivity and caring you have for each other. And that's more what the experience of adoration is like, for me at least. Yes, there are the big moments. But they're relatively few. The little moments of peace, just being still and knowing he is God—that's really the fountain that you're drinking from in adoration.

Did you read Scripture and spiritual books to help increase your awareness of his presence?

Yes. A lot of reading. One of the books I read very early on was a collection of letters from one priest to a brother priest. I don't remember the title, but the letters were about eucharistic adoration. And the things that he said in there—a lot of them were quotes from saints and modern holy people like Mother Teresa—he would talk about Jesus being so happy to see us when we come in to adore him. "Jesus is smiling," he said, "just overjoyed to see us coming to be with him." That book helped put me at ease; it put holy thoughts and images in my mind, and that helped me very much with my prayer. It made it much easier to pray in the adoration chapel. Remember: I was very nervous about the whole thing at first, very afraid I would do something wrong in there.

And now you're more at home there than anywhere else.

Yes, including my own home, in a way. I used to do most of my praying in my bedroom, but now, I go to the chapel, where Jesus is just a few feet in front of you and you're never interrupted. Not only after daily Mass, but lots of times I'll fill in for people who cancel when they're sick or away or whatever.

Has your and your husband's love for adoration caught on with your children?

Our chapel has a beautiful stained-glass window of the Sacred Heart of Jesus. At night, from outside, the window is all lit up. It's a beautiful reminder that Jesus is in there. Every time we drive past it, I say, "Hi Jesus! I love you!" The kids know that I do, and I think my faith helps them to believe, too. In fact, they often make a holy hour with us. On their own, they take it upon themselves to pray the rosary or read the great spiritual books in our chapel.

Given what you now know about the real presence of Christ in the Eucharist, what would you say to someone who right now is lost and thinking, "Religion is fine for some people, but not for me"? Well, I began thirsting for souls when I fell in love with Jesus, and I cannot tell you the things that happened. I just can't begin to tell you.

I'll just give you one example. One morning I was in adoration, after daily Mass, thinking about a beautiful talk our pastor had recently given. He had quoted from Mother Teresa; he talked about the prayer the Missionaries of Charity pray each morning, the one about being Jesus to other people: "Take everything I am and have and replace it with you, Jesus, so that everybody who sees me knows you and loves you"—that kind of thing.

Now I pray that prayer myself every morning, my own version of it. I've been doing so for a long time. But this particular day I had a book with that exact prayer in it; I prayed that prayer in the chapel and thought about Father's talk and ... this is the thing that kills me. God works immediately sometimes. He is so unbelievable when we turn our hearts over to him in love and ask him for the right things. This foolish, frightened person—me—was going into situations, asking Jesus to take care of them. And miraculous things were happening.

Well, this particular day, I left the chapel, got in my car and drove down the street to the drugstore to pick up a few things. I saw a few elderly ladies and I thought to myself: "Most of the people in the world feel unloved, or not loved enough; they have angry looks on their faces because they've had to harden themselves against the meanness in the world." I've often struck up conversations with the ladies there just because of praying the Mother Teresa prayer, given them a smile, and you can't believe the beautiful conversations I've had. A smile just opens up people's hearts like you can't believe.

Anyway, that day, after coming out of the chapel and praying that prayer, and having a chat with some of these elderly ladies, I'm at the cash register to pay for my purchases. It's very slow; very few people are in the store just then—which, in itself, is a little unusual at that store. There's a woman in front of me. Middle-aged, maybe just a little yuppie-ish. Well-off. She's giving the cashier, also a middle-aged woman, a hard time. Really pressing her on some product or some price—as if the cashier has anything to do with it. So I'm thinking, "Oh, that poor lady." And I say a quick prayer for her as I'm waiting my turn in line.

It got to be my turn. I put my stuff on the counter and the cashier kept her head down, as though she couldn't bring herself to look up at me. She said, very softly, "Pardon me—are you a Christian?" And I said, "Yes." And she said, "I mean, are you really a Christian? Do you love Jesus?" And I said, "Oh, yes." And she said, "I thought so. You were in here last week and you were the only one who was kind to me." She said, "Would you please pray for me? I'm going through menopause and I feel like I can't keep this job anymore. I don't know what I'm going to do." I told her, "Yes, I will pray for you." She still looked distressed, but she also looked clearly relieved by that little exchange of kindness and faith.

And then I went out to the parking lot and there was a young woman I know from church—somebody who no longer goes to our church. I said, "Hi, how are you doing?" She looked troubled, and she said, "Can you talk to me? I really need to talk to someone who can tell me that God is real." So I get in her car and she's telling me how her life is falling apart; she has a wonderful husband but she's in love with her boss. She knows she's doing the wrong thing but there's a tremendous pull on her heart to go the wrong way and she doesn't know how to deal with it. She says she left the Church over some silly argument she had with the pastor. And she's tried a whole bunch of other churches but hasn't found Jesus. And on and on and on she goes.

I looked at her and I said, "Yes—God is real. And, boy did you come to the right person!" I told her my whole story and then I said, "The first thing you need to do is quit your job and get away from that man who is breaking your marriage apart." We continued to talk and talk and talk.

The point is, I use this one day as an example, but it really wasn't out of the ordinary at all. These kinds of things have happened to me everywhere I go since I fell in love with Jesus in the Eucharist—and especially since I began praying my own version of the Mother Teresa prayer, praying to God to let me be the means by which others come to Jesus.

Earlier you described your present prayer life as dry and, from the way you described it, unrewarding. How is it that you're in a state of dryness and full of zeal for eucharistic adoration at the same time?
My experience of falling in love with Jesus was so strong for a good year afterward that it really carries me through to this day. It was a time of miraculous things happening every day. Every day. There was not a place I could go and not have God give me some sign of his presence in my life and his love for me.

One of my favorite spiritual books is *He and I*, by Gabrielle Bossis. It's really been a help. In that book, Jesus says: "Ask me to take care of all the small details of your life, even the little things that make life miserable. All your fears and all your anxieties." Well, I was certainly full of those. I mean, I was nervous about everything, afraid to do anything.

Whether it was going to my daughter's school, or walking into church in front of a crowd, going to a basketball game—just everything. And, suddenly, when Jesus entered my life in a major way, that all changed.

So eucharistic adoration has helped you become a calmer, more peaceful person.

More peaceful, yes. Even though I may not look perfectly calm on the outside, I may look no different than I ever did, inside I know Jesus is running the show, and that puts me at ease.

One other thing I have to say is that it's not just about what you can get out of eucharistic adoration that's such a blessing. It's also what you can give.

When I first started going to adoration, I realized that, not only was I benefiting from Jesus' presence, but he rejoiced in my being with him. I knew he was getting joy out of my being there with him.

Now there was something I never could have said before—that I could give God joy. But I believe it with all my heart now. And that keeps me going, too. It's an incentive to persevere because I remember that I'm not just doing something for myself, out of my own neediness. I'm doing it because, in a certain sense, God needs me. His love and desire for me is so strong that, in the same way people in love say this about the one they're in love with, he needs me.

What would you like the world to know about eucharistic adoration?

Two main things, I think. One, that God deserves our adoration. Jesus present in the Eucharist is such an unbelievable gift, one he left us until the end of time. And he should be loved and adored, always. That's the most important thing, I think.

The other thing, and it's far behind in second place, is what it does for the person doing the adoring. You can't find greater consolation, assistance, reassurance, help—a greater *experience* of God's presence—than you find in the Eucharist.

I believe that the reason Jesus gives himself to us in this way is to assist us through life as we make our way toward him for all eternity, to make us holy now so we can make it to heaven and be with him more fully in eternity. Along the way, as we grow in holiness, we become better sons, daughters, mothers, fathers, friends, neighbors and so on.

I've never been a good wife, mother, neighbor, friend without the eucharistic Jesus in my life. Before my conversion experience, I wasn't a blessing to anyone. Maybe by today's standards I was better than I give myself credit for, but then today's standards are pretty low. Now I know what God wants from me. And I don't always succeed in doing it, but I try.

I have to think that the progress that I've made in my life with God has to be due in great part to the gift of the Eucharist, and a huge part of that is eucharistic adoration. Adoration is secondary to Communion, of course, but for me the two have become more than just complementary; they're inseparable. Just the thought that no matter what time of day it is, whenever you feel moved or need help, you can go there and tell Jesus everything. And nothing is asked of you. He is just always available.

Even when we don't perceive his availability, as you are struggling with now?
Yes. It's the struggle that matures us, that teaches us to walk by faith rather than sight.

I think that until people experience God answering their prayers, his physical presence among us is hard to believe. Even then, the first time, it's like, "That was wonderful, but it could have been a coincidence." The second time, whoa! Then, as your whole life changes, it's like, "This is incredible. What was I waiting for?" This is why people become fanatical sometimes, go off the deep end and become so-called Jesus freaks. You just can't contain yourself when he starts working in your life.

I mean, could there be any better news than the fact that this world and all its troubles is not the end? And that there is somebody who is absolute love and you are going to live in eternal bliss with him forever? And that everything you've done wrong can be forgiven? And he'll help you along the way to make it to him?

That's the good news—the Gospel. There isn't better news than that. See, I believe that anybody who goes and spends time with Jesus in the Blessed Sacrament is going to find it difficult to keep his or her mouth shut about our wonderful Jesus, even if that person wants to.

God will prove himself to you. It's unfortunate that he has to, but in the world we live in, the way we've become hardened with sin, our hearts closed to God, he will go out of his way to prove himself to you. The cross was way out of his way. He's still going out of his way for us. The least we can do, to return the favor, is go out of our way a little bit to be with him. I'm going to keep doing that every chance I get— no matter how I feel.

CHAPTER 6

Tim

"Down in adoration falling, this great Sacrament we hail;...
Faith will tell us Christ is present when our human senses fail."

St. Thomas Aquinas (1225–74)

Another interview, another incredible testimony. I'm starting to get spoiled.

Tim, a thirty-four-year-old journalist, is a convert from a mainline Protestant denomination. Like Dylan and Mal, the other converts with whom I spoke, Tim has a eucharistic witness that's closely tied up with his life's story.

In other words, like them, he saved me the trouble of sifting through pages of notes to write an introduction to his section.

You don't want to miss the story of how Tim and his wife, Mary, welcomed their fourth child into the world on Tim's birthday—and why Tim experienced the occasion as an unmistakable sign of God's grace at work in his life. It's truly astonishing.

I'm also a sucker for a good conversion story, and Tim's is an excellent one because it came about through much struggle, prayer and study. Ultimately, his embrace of the Catholic faith had everything to do with his recognizing the real presence of Jesus in the Blessed Sacrament.

(Full disclosure: Tim is a friend and a colleague of mine. But, going into this conversation, I knew very little of what drew him into the Catholic faith, let alone the details of his conversion or his family history.)

"The Eucharist really was central to my conversion," Tim told me. "I *was a good, practicing Lutheran at the time; my wife was a Catholic. I had come to an understanding of most other Catholic doctrines through a class I took on the fundamentals of the Catholic faith at a nearby parish."*

I signed up for the class because I was interested in how the two churches were different beneath the surface.

Some Sundays we'd go to both my Lutheran and her Catholic church. I could really see that, even though the worship was very similar—the liturgy was very close and even the Scripture readings were often the same—there was a difference in how the Catholics practiced Communion.

For one thing, in the Lutheran church, you might have Communion only once a month, depending on what kind of Lutheran you are. Growing up, my family practiced the Lutheran faith, but we weren't particularly devout. We would miss church on Sunday without thinking much about it, and it wasn't unusual for two or three months to go by without receiving Communion. And so the thing that became obvious to me was that in the Lutheran church the focus is really on the Word—both Scripture and the homily—whereas, in the Catholic Church, you've got Scripture, a homily and *Communion* every single Sunday. In fact, of course, every single day if you choose to go to daily Mass—which is something I've been doing for some time.

So it was clear to me that there was a real difference there, and I found that intriguing.

Coming from that background, how did the idea of *praying* before the Eucharist, let alone receiving it more often, strike you?

I was actually quite open to it. I'm somewhat of a lazy pray-er; I knew that I needed more prayer time in my life.

What happened was, my wife's parish instituted perpetual adoration and my wife was one of the coordinators to set it up. She was responsible for one day of the week; she had to try to find people to fill out the twenty-four hours of that day—twenty-four hours, twenty-four people. It seemed very natural for me to volunteer, even though, at the time, I had no idea what eucharistic adoration was. All I knew was that it meant committing to one hour a week to prayer in this "adoration chapel" they had, whatever that was. I thought, "that's not too much to give back to God."

It wasn't like I suddenly came to a deep understanding of what the Eucharist was. But it sure didn't take long once I started going every Sunday night.

What was your impression the first time you walked into the chapel, still a Protestant, and saw the exposed Host up there?
I think it struck me, initially, as a little bit odd, in that I didn't have a full understanding of what that consecrated Host was. You know, the monstrance was up there, and it's ornate and quite beautiful. I don't think I knew enough to genuflect that first time, let alone get on both knees whenever the Host is exposed—one knee is the norm when it's reserved in the tabernacle. I'm pretty sure I just went in there and sat down. And I think I probably did a little bit of spiritual reading and spent most of the time in prayer.

And yet, even on that first night, there was an incredible calm that came over me. I believe I was alone, as I usually am during my hour, which is 10 to 11 P.M. on Sundays.

How long ago was that?

It was in September 1994. It was a Sunday. We had Mass; Archbishop Harry Flynn came and instituted perpetual adoration. They processed into this side chapel with the monstrance. And so my first time going to adoration would have been that evening.

And you've gone every week since then?

Yes, with a few exceptions, like when we've been out of town. It's really been beautiful. And it was really key to my conversion. Over time, going to adoration week after week, the peace and the calm and the quality of my conversation with God—it gradually came to me whom, instead of what, I was kneeling before in there.

I don't remember at what precise point the understanding began to sink in, but before long I began to genuflect before the tabernacle and to kneel before the exposed Host. And this came even before the Eucharist had really been explained to me. It was just the growing realization that this is Christ I'm in here with.

Now, sure, I saw people doing what they do before they get into the pew at Mass—but, let's face it, quite a few don't genuflect so much as just sort of dip slightly. [Laughs.] And then, it's hard to tell what they're motioning toward. Only a few seem to get right down on one knee, facing the tabernacle—bowing to Jesus—when they come into church. All these years later, I sometimes wish the priest would spell genuflection out a little more clearly from time to time. Remind people how to do it, and what we're doing by it, and why we do it. Because Jesus is Lord, that's why!

And now, when I'm in adoration, I remain on my knees for much, if not most, of the hour. And I really compare this growing awareness for me to the disciples on the road to Emmaus in Luke 24. Think of those disciples. They're impressed by this stranger, and he opens up Scripture to them, explains it to them—and they still don't recognize him. Really, that's exactly how I was as a Lutheran. I thought I knew Christ, because I knew his Word. I knew Scripture very well. But it was truly in the breaking of the bread that, in retrospect, I have really come to know him. And adoration has been an integral part of that.

Other doctrines, devotions and sacraments played a crucial role in my conversion, especially the Sacrament of Reconciliation. But it was really through eucharistic adoration, I think, that my conversion became inevitable. Because once I knew the truth about the Eucharist, I couldn't wait to receive him. Everything fell into place; I went to the pastor and told him: "I cannot wait!" I felt I had been denying Christ in some sense. And so I came in.

You mentioned earlier that you've kept a journal ever since you started with adoration. Can you tell me about that?
I think it was my first Easter as a Catholic that I started using some of the time in adoration for writing. Specifically, I began recording prayers. It started as a prayer journal, and it's become sort of an ongoing letter to Christ—prayers, petitions, praises and just thoughts I've shared with him while in adoration. It's been almost seven years now, and I've got all of it right here, in a three-ring binder. It's still growing strong, I guess you could say.

It's interesting. When you said you'd be calling, I went back to look through some of the things I've written down. My spiritual odyssey through the years is laid out in all these pages. Most of it is too personal to publish, but it's helpful to me because sometimes it's easy to feel as though you haven't made much progress in your spiritual life, and this shows me otherwise. It provides real encouragement to persevere.

It's beautiful to go back and see where I was when I was still pretty new to the Catholic faith. And one of the things that really strikes me, when I go back and look at what I wrote down in 1995, 1996, 1997, is that a lot of my big prayer requests have been answered. One of the things that's in there over and over again from those early years is a petition to God to grant me direction concerning my job. To look now and see the work I'm doing—using my writing skills for the Church—it's very clear that prayer has been answered. And those prayers for direction concerning my job have been replaced by other things on my mind and in my heart.

There was also a long run of praying to start a family. Well, my wife and I had some complications with pregnancies, and today we have four beautiful children. I look back at the entries when Mary was pregnant, with twins in one pregnancy, and I can see how God was there through it all.

So many of my prayers, as I check back, have been answered. Of course, some haven't—or, at least, not in the way I was hoping for. And there are some things I see going all through these years that I'm sure I'll be praying for my whole life—the conversion of family members and things of that nature. But it really is awesome to see how many have been answered.

Where does the journaling fit in with the rest of your routine?
My turn with Jesus now is 9 to 10 P.M. on Sunday nights. The first fifteen minutes or so, I spend in prayer. The second fifteen minutes is when I do the journaling. And then I usually read, either from the Bible or from whatever spiritual book I might be reading at the time. And then, the remaining time, the final part, is back to prayer. I kind of wrap the hour in prayer, with writing and reading in the middle. We

usually say the rosary every day at home, as a family, but if we've missed it that day, I'll say it in adoration.

It's impressive that you've kept up not only with adoration but also journaling for seven years.

I don't know how I'd get by without either. That's how I came to know Christ.

It's funny. I was listening to a radio talk show recently. A woman called in and said the Catholic Church doesn't support people having a personal relationship with Christ. I had to just laugh at that, because it's a personal relationship with Christ that I specifically *have* found as a Catholic. Through adoration and daily Mass, in particular, I feel I've really come to know him on a much deeper level than I ever did before.

And that very personal relationship, that intimacy with God, is what sustains me in my faith, my life, my work, my role as husband and father. I can't imagine not going to daily Mass and weekly adoration. I can't imagine not having that intimate relationship with God. The relationship I have with Christ today through the Eucharist has come to be the most important and precious thing in my life.

You feel the Eucharist, which is silent, enables you to have a deeper personal relationship with Christ than you had with him strictly through his Word, which is discursive?

Well, I'm glad we don't have to choose between God's Word and his Word made flesh. I'm glad we don't have to separate the two, or choose one over the other. But, if you pressed me, I'd have to say yes to that question.

Why?

I think it's just that Christ humbled himself to become a man and to give us himself, all of us for all generations following his incarnation, in this sacrament. It's so beautiful; you can just sit and contemplate the awesomeness of that humility for hours. That we are able to receive Christ into our bodies and to sit with him, in close physical proximity. Isn't that proximity, that intense intimacy, the deepest and central meaning of Communion? If you don't have that every week at least, you certainly aren't going to have the kind of connection he invites you to have with him.

Was it Aristotle who said that, in order to become friends with someone, you need to spend time with him or her? I mean, that's really all you're doing in eucharistic adoration. You're going before the Lord and spending time with him.

As a Protestant, you understood Scripture and sermons to be the core of your life in Christ. Was the shift in focus a major adjustment for you?

Not really. Or if it was, it came very naturally to me, for some reason. Scripture is God's Word, but the Eucharist is God. Just as you can get to know a friend pretty well through the letters that person writes you, you can get to know a whole lot about God through the Scripture. But you can get to *know* him only through being *with* him. The Eucharist isn't the only way to be with him—you can be in his presence anywhere, through prayer—but it is the way he gave us to be most physically close to him. To actually be with him.

It's hard to understand why people think there's an "either/or" proposition with regard to Scripture and the Blessed Sacrament. I mean, I always have my Bible with me in adoration, and there are plenty of Bibles there for anyone who comes in. I certainly read Scripture while in adoration, and most people I know do the same.

How do you know the Eucharist is Jesus?
That's what Jesus himself said. It's right there in John 6 and in the Gospel accounts of the Last Supper. And that's what the Church has taught from its earliest days.

That's a sound answer. But it's also a safe one, and I'm not going to let you off the hook that easy. Don't you sometimes wrestle with any doubts, given our cultural proclivity ever since the Enlightenment to trust our senses over our faith?
No. I really don't. And I don't see how it could come to that for me because coming to faith in the Church as the Mystical Body of Christ, and to the Eucharist as the body, blood, soul and divinity of Christ, was such a long, hard struggle for me. Once I took that step, I don't see where there's any chance of going back on it, rethinking it.

It was as if, at some point when I was considering the teachings of the Catholic Church, Jesus asked me the exact same question he asked his disciples in John 6:67. After he explained that you had to eat his flesh and drink his blood in order to have eternal life, a lot of them said, "This is a hard saying; who can accept it?" And the Gospel tells us that it was then that many who had been following him left him. He turned to the disciples who were still with him and asked, "Do you also want to leave?" Of course, it was St. Peter who said, "To whom will we go? You have the words of eternal life; we are convinced that you are the Holy One of God."

Through the process of my conversion, God brought me to pretty much that same point. Once you say yes to God, when he's made it very clear what it is he's asking you to do and believe, you can't very well go back and change your mind. Or I guess you could, if you don't mind living a lie.

Do the Lutherans have anything like eucharistic adoration?

Not that I ever heard of. It might be because of the way they understand what the Holy Spirit does at the consecration. Where Catholics believe the bread and wine *become* the body of Christ while retaining the appearance of bread and wine, Lutherans believe the bread and wine remain bread and wine while also taking on the substance of Christ's body and blood.

What made that less convincing for you than Catholic theology on the Eucharist?

Two things. One, either a change occurs or it doesn't. Jesus didn't say, "Take and eat; this bread *contains* my body." Nor, by the way, did he say, "This bread *represents* my body," which is the way most evangelical Protestants understand it. He said, "*This is my body.*"

The second thing is that the Church's authority became apparent to me overall, so I wasn't going to pick one doctrine from one church and another from somewhere else. Either the Church is apostolically authoritative or it's not. I came to accept that it is.

There's also a verse in Hebrews in which the writer says, "Jesus Christ is the same yesterday, today and forever." It might be easier to see that reality in the Eucharist, the appearance of which hasn't substantially changed since the Last Supper, than in preaching, which clearly has. For example, many preachers today boil the Gospel down to, "Have you accepted Jesus as your personal Lord

and Savior?" That way of characterizing Christian discipleship was unheard of before our times; it's clearly a reflection of the modern tendency to view the human will primarily in psychological terms. That's an interesting point, and I think it's very relevant to this discussion. Jesus is the same yesterday, today and forever. The Eucharist is Jesus. Therefore the Eucharist is the same yesterday, today and forever. I like that.

We've had the Eucharist since the Last Supper, when Jesus instituted it as a way to be truly with us, as he promised, until the end of time. And it hasn't changed one iota—unleavened bread and wine.

The Church's understanding of the sacrament has grown; adoration really didn't start for a few centuries and finally became a normal part of the Church's life in the early 1200s, when St. Francis championed eucharistic devotion. But you're sitting there, your temporal body surrounded by temporal things—including the monstrance, beautiful and consecrated though it is in its own right—and there's the Eternal One, the Holy Immortal One, right in front of you. And isn't it ironic that the Host seems so fragile and we seem so strong, at least while we're still young and relatively healthy, and yet the reality is exactly the other way around? If you look at the Mass, during the sacrifice of the Mass, heaven really touches earth. The Eucharist is literally a piece of heaven on earth. And this is especially evident to our senses in perpetual eucharistic adoration; I believe that's why parishes that have it are really blessed. We can go and be with Jesus, face to face, anytime; in perpetual adoration he is a perpetual companion here on earth.

There are really three ways that Christ gives himself to us eucharistically. One, of course, is as victim, in the holy sacrifice of the Mass.

Two, Communion, which is really food for our souls. And then third, reserved in the tabernacle or exposed for adoration, he is there as a perpetual companion, always there for us to draw near to his side.

A lot of very down-to-earth, nonfanatical people are having very transcendent, mystical, religious experiences in eucharistic adoration chapels. They're retreating from the world for a while, as Jesus withdrew for a while, while at the same time entering more deeply into the world—becoming more realistic, more concerned for the welfare of other people's souls, and bringing all that right to Jesus. Adoration is definitely a mini-retreat. And it can be a very intense one. Intensely peaceful; at times intensely illuminating. How many of us take the time for prayer? Speaking for myself, I can tell you that I often do not take the time I ought to and need to for prayer. How often do we go and sit with the Lord? And anyone can do that in any Catholic Church in which Christ is reserved in the tabernacle—which is every Catholic church, unless it's been closed and decommissioned.

How is your prayer before the Blessed Sacrament different from, say, your prayer at home with the rosary?
It's much more conversational, usually. More like I'm engaged in an impromptu chat with Jesus. I'm not saying I hear his audible voice. But, mind you, I have had some startling revelations while before the Blessed Sacrament.

I really haven't talked with too many people about this ...

That's about to change!
I'll try ... We lost our first child to miscarriage. I remember bringing that quite often, early on, in prayer before the Blessed Sacrament. At

the time, I was still very new to the faith and to eucharistic adoration. Brand new. I remember this being a very difficult thing to go through, and praying a lot about it.

One of the things that made it particularly difficult was that a lot of our friends were having children. And I thought about this child that we had lost. I thought, here's this child that I'll never be able to meet. At least, not in this life. I really grieved; sometimes I still continue to grieve over that loss.

So I remember bringing that in prayer to Jesus in the Blessed Sacrament quite often. And I remember one night ... Because I did not get to meet this child, and I so much wanted to know, for one thing, was it a boy or a girl? And it was in prayer one evening, in adoration, that I was just struck with the strongest impression that the child was a boy, and I was struck with the name Gabriel. And that was very helpful for me in the grieving process because I was able to think of the child, and name him, which my wife and I then did. And it gave us a person that we could mourn.

So that was one thing that came out of adoration for me very early. And there have been some other things.

Can you talk about them?
Sure. Some of them.

My scheduled hour is Sunday night from nine to ten. There is a powerhouse of prayer there when I walk in. Some of the people I consider to be—I don't want to use the word *holy* because I don't want to set them up on a pedestal—but they are the holiest people I know. I walk into the adoration chapel and there are usually three other people there. Usually one leaves shortly after I arrive and then the other two leave a bit after. They're all lay people. I've gotten to know them over the years, and I just really respect and am inspired by these three individuals. There's a bond there between the four of us somehow. Even though we seldom acknowledge one another in the chapel, out of respect for Jesus exposed, let alone speak to one another—though we are friends and do speak quite often, outside of adoration.

And my wife, Mary, says the same thing about daily Mass. We go to a different parish for daily Mass than Sunday Mass because of scheduling, and there is this bond that you know is there with these people you worship with every day—even though, again, we rarely speak to one another. You see the same faces each day, there to worship and receive Jesus, and a bond forms. You might not know it to observe all of us there in daily Mass, but I'll bet if you were to ask the others who go every day, they'd say they feel the same way.

You had another story you were going to tell me?
Oh, yes. In early December 1999, I was in adoration, and this woman who followed me on the schedule came in. We normally didn't talk to one another in the chapel—no one talks in the chapel; people really respect the need for silence in the presence of our Lord exposed—but for some reason, I remember looking over at her and she just gave me a look like she wanted to say something. She told me she and her husband had just found out they were expecting. And what's remarkable about this is that, for years before that, they had been unable to conceive. And she told me that she had gone to Confession and expressed her frustration over this to the priest. The priest asked if she'd like him to give her a special blessing. And I think it was just a couple of weeks later that she found out she was pregnant.

So she came in and told me this little story, and it was wonderful. Because I had known from previous conversations outside of the chapel that this couple was trying to have a child. The thing was, Mary and I were trying to conceive, too. And we'd been having a difficult time of it. The next day, I told Mary about the woman's story. And Mary said, "Hey, that's a great idea—we should have the associate pastor bless us one morning after daily Mass." And so we scheduled a date; it was sometime before Christmas. We went back and the priest said a special blessing for both of us. We use Natural Family Planning, so we always know when we conceive. And it was right around Christmas that we found out we were expecting; the projected due date was September 13, which is my birthday—in 2000, the Jubilee Year, no less.

Anyway, I had this feeling all along, from the very beginning of our marriage, that God was going to bless us with a child on my birthday.

You mean you expected not only to become a father but also to have a child born on your birthday?

Yes, because of the circumstances of my own conception.

You were conceived under unusual circumstances?

I'm not sure if *unusual* is the right word, unfortunately. The fact is, my father wanted to have me aborted.

Whoa. That sounds like a story waiting to be told.

It is. It's a whole separate story. I can tell you about it in a minute. But because of that, I just knew that God would give us a child on my birthday. Because it would say something to my parents about the fact that, you know, my mother carried me to term, and had me, and now here, how many years later, we would have a baby on my birthday ...

And so September 13, 2000, came—and sure enough, we had Elena Grace. To me, it was just such a testament to life. I was thinking, had I not been here, she wouldn't be here.

And, yes, I credit that, to a great extent, to eucharistic adoration. Because I was in adoration when this woman came in and told me about the blessing and her subsequent pregnancy. And that provoked us to go and seek out a blessing, which seemed to lead to the birth of our fourth child.

Coincidence or miracle?

I have no way of knowing for sure, but I'm a man of faith, and it would be hard for me to look at that turn of events and not see God's hand guiding them.

What about your own birth?

Well, my parents were married quite young. Right after they were married, my father, who was in the service, was sent to Guam for eighteen months or so. When he came home, my mother was six months pregnant. She had had an affair. And my dad strongly urged her to have an abortion. Thankfully, she refused. And I came along.

The thing is, this was not told to me until I was twenty-five—just eight years ago. My father came to me and told me he wasn't my biological father. Talk about having the rug pulled out from under you! And then I was told the whole story of how I was conceived and how I was almost aborted.

Were you angry at your mom for not telling you all this sooner?

Yeah, there was some anger at first. But then, as I talked to her, she explained that there just had never been a good time to tell me. And I could understand that. I could see how difficult it must have been for her. There was some embarrassment on her part, I'm sure.

I'll bet you've brought this before the Blessed Sacrament!
For a while after all this was brought to light, quite a while, yeah. Not so much now, though. God made his statement by having our daughter born on my birthday. That said everything, for me. Now I'm on to other things.

Tim, it must have been an upheaval for you to find out, at twenty-five years old, that your dad is not really your father.
Oh, yeah.

So I'd love to know how you've been able to work that through, especially through your prayer life before the Blessed Sacrament.
Well, the way it's worked its way out is ... I've learned how true it is that the truth will set you free.

In learning the truth about my father, I have been led to a far greater truth: The Church of Christ, the Catholic Church, really is the Mystical Body of Christ. And he really does work in amazing ways through it.

See, all of this happened about the time that I was debating coming into the Church. And what happened was, I needed a convert to talk to. I needed someone who understood where I was coming from as a Lutheran, with all my questions about, and objections to, the Catholic faith. My wife couldn't provide perspective because she's a cradle Catholic. She didn't have the same questions I had.

Well, God provided someone, and in a very unique way. It was all connected with this revelation about my father. What happened was, after I found out who my biological father was, I learned that I also had two half-brothers. And about a month after all this came out, I met one of my half-brothers. His name is Rich. Walking into the restaurant where we were meeting, it was just remarkable. He's about thirteen years older than I am, and it was like looking in a mirror and seeing what I was going to look like thirteen years later. It was incredible how much alike we look.

As we sat down over dinner, here it comes out that, at age eighteen, he converted—from Lutheran to Catholic! So just at that moment when I needed a convert from Lutheranism to talk to, God provided one—and one with some amazing extras, at that. He was a true brother in more ways than one. I just thought that was so phenomenal, and so clearly by the hand of God, that my own conversion was at that point really a done deal.

I certainly have taken all of this before the Lord in adoration. Early on, after the truth of this came out, it really looked as if my parents were going to divorce. I think the cat being out of the bag was a factor in that. This was something they had been suppressing all these years. So I was praying about that every week. And my parents, praise God, are still together.

Did you get to meet your biological father?
I got to meet him only once. He was an alcoholic. Less than a year after I met him, he died of cirrhosis of the liver. That was in 1993. He didn't have an awful lot to say, but it was good to meet him. I realized that the only connection we shared was genetic. I mean, he took no responsibility for me whatsoever. Yet it was good, just getting to meet my father.

And your dad was your dad, as far as you knew all those years.

Yeah. There had been some misdirected hostility there through the years. He said a lot of things to me that, as his son, I always wondered why a father would say to his son. He was a little hostile toward me from time to time. Yet he provided a loving home and for the most part raised me as his own.

How did your parents feel about your becoming Catholic?

They're pretty nominal Lutherans, so it wasn't a big deal. My mother cried. Although I really try to tell her that I'm thankful for what she gave me, because without the foundation they gave me—prayer, Scripture, pointing me toward faith in Christ—I wouldn't be where I am today.

Looking back through your prayer journal, what do you notice has changed about your prayer?

Well, one thing I notice is that I used to repeat my petitions over and over again. I think that, having so many prayers answered over the years, big and small, I've grown to trust the Lord more than ever. I don't see myself repeating petitions the way I once did. I'll make the petition, consider the matter in God's hands and let it go at that. If it's God's will for my request to be answered, it will be.

Also, I find that I am more charismatic, if I may use that term loosely. By that I mean that I was never very good at spontaneous prayer. But I find that, as the years have gone on, I am better able to do that kind of prayer. Not only praying more freely and conversationally but also just praising God spontaneously. I suppose you could say that my personality is rather reserved. But now I will find that, some evenings in adoration, especially if I'm there alone, I will do that. You know—

"Praise God!" or "Alellujah!" Sometimes that's all I'm able to say, but at certain times, that about says it all. Just letting the Spirit move me in the moment more—that's something I never really did before.

What else do you see as you look back through your journal?
More spiritual maturity. I find that I'm praying less for my own needs and more for the needs of others. Looking back through my journal entries, it's almost embarrassing how much of the early entries were about me, me, me. That has definitely changed, I am glad to report.

Also the depth of the conversation I'm able to have with God. One of the things I find so beautiful about the Catholic faith is just the richness and the depth there. It seems the more I learn, the more there is to learn. And I see that sort of reflected in my prayer journal. In the beginning, I may have understood the basics of the faith, but my understanding was sort of elementary.

So really, there's just been a lot of growth. I wouldn't say I understand God more, because that would be presumptuous, but I appreciate the infinite depth of his mystery more, if that makes any sense.

What is the interior experience like? Can you describe it?
Sometimes it seems like you enter a kind of zone. I guess you could call it the God Zone. Not all the time, but sometimes. And when it happens, you know it happens.

What's it like?
I don't know; it's indescribable.

Oh, good—then this part of the interview won't take very long at all.

[Laughs heartily.] It's peaceful, it's beautiful. It's ... I don't know ... I'm afraid of sounding New Agey by trying to put it in words.

Come on—you're a writer. Give it a shot.

Well, it's almost a feeling as if you are outside of yourself, in a sense. And yet there is a communion, a oneness with the Lord that I find once in a while. You're not speaking any words, but yet you're having a conversation.

Now, I know that doesn't make any sense, but again, I don't know that I can put words to it.

What precipitates this happening when it does happen?

I have no idea. I don't know why sometimes I'll reach that place with the Lord and other times I won't. But it doesn't happen terribly often. To be honest, sometimes I actually fall asleep. I don't know if I should admit to that! But it does happen once in a while. I remember, back in the beginning, the first time I dozed off in adoration, I just felt so bad about it. And I told someone about it, and that person said, "Don't worry about it—you were getting a Son tan! Sometimes there's nothing like just basking in the radiance of Christ's presence." I think the bottom line is, you shouldn't make a habit of sleeping through adoration, but you also shouldn't beat yourself up if it happens on occasion. Jesus knows how busy we are and how weary we get with our day-to-day concerns, so would he mind our resting for a while in his shadow?

What have been the exterior manifestations of God's grace flowing into your life through eucharistic adoration?

I would say I've seen it mostly within my family, in my relationships with my wife and our children.

There have been times in the past where, because of a job I was working on or whatever the pressing concern of the time happened to be, I was not really present for my family, as a husband and a father. And now I find that—and I have to attribute this at least in part to my devotion to Jesus in the Eucharist—there is much more balance in my relationships with God, with my family and with my work. And that really has been a blessing.

The other thing I have noticed is that, because I'm spending that time with Jesus every week, there is not much my conscience can get away with. If you scream at your kids, you're going to feel it as a hurdle or a disturbance in adoration. Your sins, even the little ones, will upset your peace, and, since adoration is the most deeply peaceful part of your week, that's when all those little things you've done, or said, or failed to do or say, start ringing in your ears. I think you'll probably find that eucharistic adorers are fastidious about getting to Confession fairly frequently, and this is the reason. The peace you experience in adoration when you're right with God is so beautiful that you don't want anything to disturb it—and nothing can disturb it like your own sin.

I guess there's something about being there with the one who loves you so much, and is so merciful and forgiving of all your faults, that makes you want to be your very best for him. I think that's why your failings become so evident to you while you're in his presence.

Both you and your wife are very active in adoration and the life of your parish. Has the double dose of devotion in the household helped your marriage?

Yes, and that's another whole story unto itself. Early on in our marriage, we were having communication difficulties. We nearly went our separate ways. This was about a two-year period, roughly our second and third years of marriage. I look at where we were then and where we are now, and it's night and day. I think both of us have a better relationship with Christ, and that's helped us immeasurably in having a better relationship between the two of us.

You hinted earlier that you go to Confession more frequently now than when you first became a Catholic. Is that so?

Definitely, and it's not because I'm more sinful. I just feel the need to more now than I did then, and I owe that sense mainly to eucharistic adoration.

You also said adoration helps you properly dispose yourself to receive Communion. Can you tell me how?

There is such a recognition that this is Christ. When the priest or the eucharistic minister gives you the Host and says, "The Body of Christ," you really mean it when you say, "Amen." And I would never even consider receiving while in a state of mortal sin. I just could not do that anymore. Whereas in the past, I might have, I'm sorry to admit. There's just a much deeper respect for Christ in the sacrament.

One thing I need to point out: Because your own sins, even the smaller ones, become more evident to you through adoration, sometimes it can feel like you're more sinful than ever, that you haven't really made any progress in the Christian life at all. That's an illusion. You probably aren't more sinful; it's just that the light of Christ is more intense in your life. You're bringing yourself into the light, and all your imperfections, which used to be more or less shrouded in the shadows, are now in the bright light of the Son. So of course you see them better, and of course they seem more prominent than they did before. But they're not worse than they were before, just exposed to the light.

But the main thing you get from eucharistic adoration is a strong sense of God's love and mercy. You realize that he sees every one of those failings, sins, imperfections—and loves you so much all the same. Enough to send his Son to die for those sins, and enough to call you to his side for a special dose of love every week.

CHAPTER 7

Marty

"The light of natural knowledge does not show us the object of faith, since this object is unproportioned to any of the senses. Yet we come to know it through hearing, by believing what faith teaches us, blinding our natural light and bringing it into submission."

St. John of the Cross (1542–91)

Some of my sources were at least somewhat reluctant to open their hearts and their prayer life to me and my tape recorder. Not Marty. He could hardly wait to talk about Jesus—or, more to the point, what he and Jesus had been through together since Marty made a commitment to spend an hour each week in eucharistic adoration.

Marty, a husband, father of two and professional photographer, and a very active leader in Catholic youth ministry, may have been the most quietly intense person I spoke with.

Best of all for me, the man's joy was as contagious as it was palpable.

"When adoration came to our parish, I really wanted to sign up for it right away," he said. "I just knew it would add another dimension to my walk with Jesus; it would help me go deeper with him. Although I've always been pretty good about practicing my Catholic faith, I've certainly gone through various levels of commitment and various levels of spiritual depth. As a cradle Catholic who's always practiced his faith, I always felt like I had a good relationship with Jesus—but I know it takes a lifetime to get closer to God. That's what the Christian life is all about, I think."

I think my testimony is somewhat different from a lot of people's. Only in preparing to talk to you did I stop and think about what eucharistic adoration has really come to mean to me. I am the kind of person who is very well disciplined. If I say I am going to do something, I will do it. And I think what has happened to me in adoration, and it has taken my wife to help me see this, is: Because of my year and a half of discipline in sticking with adoration, I have grown spiritually more over the past year and a half than in all the rest of my life prior to adoration coming into my life.

How so?

Well, I measure growth with ease in my spiritual life—ease in doing what God is asking me to do with my life. I'm not saying it gets any easier to do what he asks, because it's so often the hard road, but that it starts to feel more and more natural.

In the past year and a half, I've been through the two hardest periods in my life—my mother dying and me starting my own business, which is a very scary thing.

Ever since I launched it, every day of my business has been like a Friday used to be in my other job. I always looked forward to Friday. I've had a tremendous amount of peace through my work as a professional photographer, and I really feel this is where God wants me to be. And therefore I don't worry every day about where the next project is going to come from. I always know it's going to come.

And I think all of these things are how God works in me as I am increasingly obedient to the promptings he gives me, which are especially clear and acute in adoration.

I go to adoration and I don't feel anything other than a tremendous sense of peace. And that's something I need in my life. It is the most peaceful, gentle, quiet place I have in my life, my time with Jesus in adoration.

You described it earlier as supernaturally peaceful.
Oh, yes—and here's one way to describe it: We have a beautiful, wooded backyard at our home. It's very peaceful, very tranquil, very serene. And yet I'd choose the adoration chapel over my backyard, even if I ever got it all to myself, which is rare when you have kids, because it is supernaturally peaceful, whereas the backyard is merely naturally peaceful. In the adoration chapel, Jesus is there, waiting for me, waiting for me to respond to him.

I've been in adoration in a lot of different ways, especially now that I've been working a lot with young people. At the overnight prayer events we have, when the priest processes with Jesus elevated in the monstrance and everyone in the huge crowd just drops to their knees in love and reverence because they know that Jesus is passing by—I love those experiences. Because, when I come back to my own adoration chapel, I think back on those times and the memories help me to realize how close Jesus is.

I really do believe that I have been blessed in my life tremendously—in my relationship with my wife, with my kids, with the community, with everyone I come in contact with. There are plenty of struggles, some of them really hard struggles, but the strength that God has given me, the ease in accepting his will, has increased many times over in the year and a half that I've been going to eucharistic adoration.

Have your circumstances changed, or have you changed?
I'm changing. Circumstances around me are changing, too, but it's because I'm changing that things seem better. It's not the other way

around. I'm changing because God has made his presence in my life more obvious to me.

Earlier you talked about counseling young people and men. Please understand that I'm playing devil's advocate when I ask you a question like this, but is there any danger in going deep into your thoughts and then coming out feeling like you've been blessed with great wisdom, maybe a little too eager to give others advice?
I think the biggest thing from adoration is you and Jesus. The biggest thing you get is for you. You get a blessing. If the blessing helps you to help other people—I don't think I've ever shared about adoration. Even my wife and I hardly talk between us about what each of us talks to Jesus about in adoration, because it's probably the most private prayer we have. But you do get what I can only call blessings. And those blessings help you in the "active" areas of your life in Christ— the parts of your life where you are, directly or indirectly, bringing people to Jesus.

I think that, while praying for wisdom, you also need to pray for humility. You need to make sure that you don't become arrogant about the blessings and graces God gives you when you love him. Scripture says, "Be not wise in your own eyes," and I think you always need to come back to that. Because as you counsel and help others who are not that far along with Jesus yet, there is a temptation to feel like you're wise. Or you're so sure that this or that is from God that you put yourself in danger of presenting yourself like some kind of sage.

What makes you so sure that the Eucharist is even Jesus?
This simple fact: I know that faith is something I cannot get except from God, and *I have it.* I can't perceive Jesus through my sight, taste,

touch, feel or smell. And yet I know he's there. Getting back to what I said earlier about supernatural peace, Jesus is in my backyard in his divinity—but he's in the adoration chapel in both his humanity *and* his divinity. Now that I think of it, I think that's really key.

I should also mention here that I always leave time to read Scripture, and I read from solid Catholic books as well. But, on the books, I have to limit myself. Because I love to read; I could easily spend an hour engrossed in a book *about* God while completely missing the opportunity to be *with* Him. I need to give God time with me, give Jesus an opportunity to go to work on me. I often pray a rosary, and say other prayers, but the main thing is to leave plenty of time to be quiet and alone with God.

Your prayer life really took off when you began with adoration a year and a half ago.

Yes, it has really taken off since then, and I can give you an example of how that has recently manifested itself outwardly, in the "active" part of my faith.

I play electric bass guitar, and I was in a rock and roll band before I got involved with adoration. We weren't crazy carousers or anything, just a bunch of old rockers who still hadn't put the music behind us. We played in some small nightclubs and at some parties, that sort of thing. But, largely through adoration, I began to realize that that gig was the unholiest thing in my life. Now, the other guys in the band thought of me as sort of the Holy Roller, the churchgoer. And I always used to give up beer for Lent, which my bandmates could never understand.

Well, soon after I started with adoration, I was asked to play in a Life Teen band, using music to minister to young people. I knew I would have to give the other band up if I was going to embrace this opportunity. And, by going to adoration, that decision really became a no-brainer. I look at my life now, and it's because of making decisions like that that I think my spiritual life has taken a quantum leap toward God.

See, in adoration I was getting this shot, this intense blast, really, of holiness. So, where nothing in the rock band was totally debauched—in fact, the guys were all married and pretty settled in with serious careers during the day—it simply became very apparent that it didn't fit for me anymore. The time came to choose between the things of God and the things of the world and, through adoration, it became crystal-clear which I needed to cleave to and which I needed to walk away from.

How do you bring your eucharistic faith into your work as a professional photographer?

No matter what you do, if you are a serious, praying Christian, your job—any job—is going to give you a chance to witness Christ to those who do not know him, or know him in a less well-formed, uncatechized way. The way you deal with people can be Christlike regardless of your particular job.

I knew a woman whose husband was dying. She was an art director at an ad agency I was doing some work for. She called me up because she knew I was a Catholic, and she knew my faith means a lot to me. I had to ask her: "Well, how did you know that?" I didn't recall ever sharing my faith with her. And she said, "Are you kidding? You've shared about it many times." I hadn't even realized.

So I think eucharistic adoration helps you to so center your life on Jesus that you can follow St. Paul's teaching to "be all things to all people" for the sake of the Gospel, for the sake of helping to "make disciples of all nations." I can't put up a big crucifix in my studio and expect people to kneel down before it. I would lose clients in a hurry. But if there's somebody in need, or someone asks a question related to life, death, sickness, big decisions and so on, I'm more than happy to mention that I wouldn't be able to face any of those things without my faith in Jesus. And I will tell them exactly what I believe, not just that I believe in *something*.

It's especially hard today for young people. Young people today are living through an incredibly hard time. If we can give them some hope and direction by sharing what God means in our lives, we must. We simply must. It is the best thing we can do for them, and the least we can do for them.

Your work keeps you right out there in the secular world, interacting with a lot of people who don't share your faith or anything close to it. Has balancing the two worlds, so to speak, become more of a challenge for you as your faith has intensified?

I'm sure that, to many people I come in contact with in the world, I'm somewhat of a religious fanatic. And so what? To me, the true measure of discipleship is how committed you are to bringing the Gospel to the world—and then, mainly by how you live, not by what you say. As St. Francis said to the brothers when he sent them out: "Go and preach the Gospel; only use words if you have to."

I don't mind telling you that I'd prefer not to be referred to as a religious fanatic or a Jesus freak. Because, to me, those things say something about me; they really don't respect the truth of the Gospel. I don't mind at all if people want to call me a man of God. And that one aspect of my prayer is eucharistic adoration, another is the rosary, and the most important one is reception of the Eucharist in Holy Mass. Plus I read the Bible, the *Catechism,* Church teachings and so on.

And by the way, if all someone did was adoration, I think that person's devotion to Jesus would be off balance. Adoration that is not informed by the teachings of the Church, Sacred Scripture and Sacred Tradition—and, especially, balanced by reception of Communion in the Mass—can come dangerously close to mere meditation. Adoration should be an aspect of your devotion to Jesus, but it should never be the only aspect.

Eucharistic adoration helps your prayer life; it helps you progress toward God. It isn't indispensable, like food and water, but it is powerfully supplemental, like a multivitamin. You know, people will resolve to get up an hour earlier each day and use that hour to pray. Some people make good on a resolution like that; most won't be able to keep it very long. Well, when you sign on for that one hour a week, you are committed. You become duty-bound to be there. And that in itself can be a powerful aid to your prayer life. It's a simple commitment, one in which you have every encouragement and consolation to help you persevere in it—and there are some costs if you neglect it.

But best of all, God will bless your commitment. That would be the main thing I would want to tell people about adoration.

And that adoration has brought the Mass alive to me; the Scriptures, too. I have a greater desire for the Mass because of adoration. Let's face it; the *Catechism* can be kind of daunting. Some of it is written a little dryly. And yet, in adoration, you develop a great hunger to know all the Church teaches, and that sends you straight to the *Catechism* and the Bible. You come to understand the *Catechism* and to appreciate its great, Christ-centered wisdom; your Bible readings come alive.

Eucharistic adoration helps me two ways, I think. Interiorly, it helps you know how loved you are; it helps you move ever closer, always closer, to the Sacred Heart of Jesus. And exteriorly, it helps you recognize and respond to the promptings of the Holy Spirit when he calls you to witness to others all that God has done for you.

Why pray at all? What good does it do you?
How do you get closer to someone you want to be friends with? By talking. Sharing. Communicating. A friend and I went out to lunch one day and sat down. We were talking very much like you and I are talking right now. And he said to me, "I go to lunch all the time with people, and it's like, who cares? We just kill the time with small talk. But right now we're sharing our hearts." And that's where we need to be with Jesus, sharing our hearts—because he will open up to us as well, and it is incredibly satisfying when he does.

And when you need prayer, like for me on the night my mother died, the most horrific night of my life ...

Could you tell me a little about that?
My mother had Lou Gehrig's disease. She had been battling it for a year. But the timing of her death came as a complete surprise. She had been in and out of the hospital but had lately been OK. We knew she was dying, but we thought she had eight months to a year of life left.

When I speak about receiving grace through adoration, it's hard to say about anything in particular, "Yes, this was adoration." But it's the whole package that comes with letting God deeper and deeper into your life—that does pay off at the times you most need God. Because the relationship is established; he is there for you to lean on, and you've learned how to lean.

My mother's death made my entire faith come to one focal point. I remember thinking to myself, "This is my faith. It either means everything to me right now, or it means nothing." And the very next thought, the prompting, really, was very comforting: It said, "It means everything." I didn't have to ask for God; I felt God was holding me up. I had never been so vulnerable to him, and he had never been so close or so reassuring.

No doubt that God used your time in adoration to shore up your faith for that moment?
Absolutely no doubt about that. And here's an important point: Adoration also can help you for the good times. Because if you go on to have worldly success, you're going to have temptations to your pride. And adoration is a very humble, and humbling, time. You're there before God, and you're going to feel humble in his presence.

Humility is a very big part of adoration. God humbles himself to come to us under the appearance of a piece of bread; and we are, in turn, incredibly humbled that he, who is all-knowing and all-powerful, has put himself in such a vulnerable, lowly place out of love for us. The creator of all that is, who could take this world of sin and death and just crumple it in his hands, comes to us in a form that is so humble that he makes himself totally vulnerable to us. Is that love, or what?

One of the most profound things that happened in my mother's sickness was, when I first found out she had this disease, when she was first diagnosed and it was sinking in for me that she was going to die, my stomach was turned inside out. It was just a solid knot. It wouldn't let up or go away. Now, this was right around the time that I started with eucharistic adoration. So my relationship with Jesus, which had already been pretty good, was coming to a new level. And I remember waking up from sleep one night and just pleading, out loud: "God, I can't do it. I can't make it through this. I can't go to work; I can hardly put two thoughts together. I give up. I just can't live with this." I mean, I was physically overwhelmed with what was going on in my stomach, and emotionally, spiritually and psychologically overwhelmed with what was happening to my mother. And just like that, that knot that had been twisting so tightly in my stomach for days loosened and then went away.

That, to me, was a minor miracle. Because I'm not exaggerating when I say this intestinal problem was knocking me down. I mean, I literally was unfit to go to work. And it was lifted from me, totally and completely, within moments of telling God I couldn't go on. I rolled over in bed and suddenly realized it was gone.

I still had months ahead of seeing my mother through this terrible illness to her inevitable end, but suddenly I had a peace with it and, thus, could help bring a sense of peace to her and the rest of my family. In fact, my relationship with my mother went to a whole new level, because she very quickly lost her voice. And what happened was, looking my mother in the eye was a whole new way of communicating. A very deep way. We would look into one another's eyes when she couldn't speak anymore, and it was like a form of contemplative prayer. A look from her was suddenly very profound, all she was able to convey without saying a word. I would look at her, she would look at me, and we were talking in a different language, on a higher plane.

So I was able to be peaceful and love her through her illness rather than being bitter and hurt and angry at God, or overcome with grief that she was suffering and dying. The strength I found in Jesus, largely by continuing to adore him throughout this time, was an amazing witness to me of God's working in my life. Because I knew for a fact that

I didn't have that kind of strength; it was God working in me, loving me through it.

That's why I need God. Because I could have been very bitter, very angry. It could have been a year of resentment toward God. And instead he made that a very prayerful, spiritual journey with my mother. And it brought me to a place in which God was able to help me learn to lean on him, trust him, and allow him into the deepest parts of my heart.

I remember that my relatives looked at me and they were dumbfounded that I was so "together," as they put it. What they meant was that I was at peace, even though I was deeply grieved to lose my mom. What they didn't see was all the devotion and hours in prayer leading up to those moments when we laid her to rest, the hours that God used to show me he was with my mother and with me.

There's no question that my mother's death has changed me. I'm a different man than I was before, more receptive to God working in my life.

What about starting the business?

Despite some jitters early on, it was very peaceful. I prayed like I did when I was getting married—please, God, let me know what you want me to do!—and what prayer does for us in our life, I think, is God doesn't so much give you precise instructions. If God gave me direct answers, then I wouldn't be giving anything; I'd just be doing what he says like a marionette.

But I prayed about it, and I prayed about it sincerely. And gradually I had tremendous peace about the decision and, as the weeks went by, in my business. Since then, I've never worried about it.

Has deeper devotion to Christ in the Eucharist helped your marriage?

My wife and I are very blessed because we share the faith. She has helped me tremendously, going through my mother's illness and death and all. I don't know how you can live with someone if you can't share your innermost thoughts and feelings, and ours are about God. Because everything else is worldly things that can be fixed with money and power. All we have to give, as husbands and wives, is what we are.

Adoration is very private, but there have certainly been times when I've come home and said to my wife, "Guess what happened to me in adoration!" And she'll do the same with me—she spends a lot of time in adoration, even more than I do.

How has your experience of Jesus in eucharistic adoration differed from what you thought it would be like when you first started with it?

I would say that I've been surprised to find how humbling it can be to sit with Jesus.

What about it makes you feel humbled?

Simple. It's God. As soon as you walk in that door, you're just a soul before Jesus. He doesn't care if you're famous or unknown, rich or poor, big or little. He doesn't care about the externals—what we accomplish and what we gather. He only cares about the heart. You realize that so acutely by spending time adoring him.

The powerful tycoon who owns two mansions and a yacht isn't any more to God than me; we're equal standing there before the Lord. Whereas you step back out of that room, and suddenly all those things seem important again. I'm not saying I think they are, but let's face it, they seem that way in the world, out on the street. Because your identity has more to do with how the world sees you; and yet, before Jesus it has everything to do with how he sees you.

So it's humbling to be in that room with Jesus. If you were before a great and good king, you would bow out of respect. You would be deeply reverent. Well, you are before such a king—the king of all kings, the king of all creation. What could be more humbling than that? The king of the universe loves me, has time for me, wants to *be with* little old me. What's cooler than that?

CHAPTER 8

Diane

"When I am before the Tabernacle, I can say only one thing to Our Lord: 'My God, you know that I love You.' And I feel my prayer does not tire Jesus; knowing the helplessness of His poor little spouse, He is content with her good will."

St. Thérèse of Lisieux (1873–97)

Diane, Jay's wife, is Catholic to the core, and in this way: She clearly lives St. James' admonition that "Faith without works is dead."

While she was courteous and respectful throughout our conversation, early on her tone of voice conveyed a measure of skepticism over what this writer guy on the phone wanted to talk about. She certainly warmed to the occasion quickly enough, providing what I thought was a reserved but powerful witness once the discussion got rolling.

And yet, like her husband, Diane, an accountant, is clearly more comfortable living her faith than talking about it.

As I said, Catholic to the core.

I understand that you're up at four in the morning one day a week, before you go in to work, to pray in silence before the Blessed Sacrament. That's no small commitment. Can you talk about what keeps you motivated?

I would say that [eucharistic adoration] has added another dimension to my faith, something that wasn't there before.

You know, you don't start off thinking that there's one thing in particular that you're going to go looking for. I didn't go and say, "Gee, I hope I can connect with God here and …"—it just happens.

You go there and you're in a quiet place with God for an hour. Plus our adoration chapel has a lot of inspirational reading—Bibles, books. I would say that, as an experience, it opens up a whole world that I wouldn't have known about if our parish hadn't offered it.

Do you have a strong sense that you are in the same room with Jesus?

Yes. You feel awestruck. It's overwhelming sometimes.

Sometimes, during the winter especially, because we go at such an early hour, we walk in while it's still black outside and then sort of emerge into the light after having spent an hour in Jesus' presence. It's like, "Wow, there's the sun rising; what a great reminder of God's presence in the universe and in our little chapel." And that alone can be very powerful. Inspiring.

I tend to be a morning person, but I never had a reason to get up at four in the morning until now. And it's actually quite an experience, being up at an hour like that when most of the rest of the world around you is asleep. And then to go in with the Lord, who is always awake—again, it's just opening up another dimension to our lives and our religious experience that we never considered before.

Have you noticed changes in each other's spiritual life? Have you noticed Jay growing spiritually?

Well, I think we both have [grown]. We've become a lot more aware of things around us, in our lives and the world, and from a different perspective. You see the power of God and where you fit in his whole plan; you see it in each other and all your interactions with people. And you just feel thankful for the gifts you receive because of your devotion.

What kinds of gifts do you receive?
Well, for example, we have two kids. Both are in college, and both have been through the various stages that kids go through on their way from the teen years through adolescence. Our daughter is a junior; our son is a sophomore. They're both normal kids, they're happy and good and we're very thankful for all that they do. Both go to Catholic colleges, and both are active with their faith in their respective school environments. And they took that on themselves. We did not push it on them at all, because we don't believe that works with faith. There's that old saying, "Faith is caught, not taught." But I do think that our example of taking an extra step with our devotions had something to do with our kids' pursuing God beyond what most of the other kids at their schools do. It's good for them to have a base in Mom and Dad's faith, but they have to be in right relationship with God on their own efforts.

My opinion is that they need to connect with God on their own, so I don't really force that issue in the sense of demanding that they become superstar Catholics. I mean, they reach an age, and they need to spread their wings. And they need to come to the realization of their need for God themselves. I think our example is more powerful than any laws we might lay down. At least, it's worked for us, because clearly they are active and involved with their faith communities at their schools. And their schools are not exactly what you would call bastions of orthodoxy, even though they are Catholic schools. So it's really on their own initiative that they're finding their way to God.

One of the reasons their spiritual development is so exciting to us is that both of them had a little trouble feeling connected at our parish. We moved into this area, and our previous parish had had a better social program for young people—more dances, a better CYO program and so on. So we went to Mass as a family and all, but I think they were participating more out of duty than a really dynamic relationship with the Lord. At the time we moved here, this parish was kind of sleepy. This was before perpetual adoration was started.

So, because they weren't all that strongly connected, when they went away to school, we were a little worried about them losing their faith. Even though they were going to Catholic colleges—you know, you hear all kinds of stories even there of kids just giving up on church altogether. So our kids' finding their faith on an even deeper level than before has been a gift.

And we think it has a lot to do with their seeing our faith in action, especially in devotions like eucharistic adoration.

In what way are they participants in their campus faith communities?

Well, they're both interested in becoming extraordinary eucharistic ministers, though that hasn't happened yet. But my daughter is just very involved with various social programs and she's a greeter at Mass. And my son, every Monday night, the church on his campus has a dinner and a spiritual growth program and he's gotten involved with that.

So they're well beyond just going out of a dry sense of duty; they certainly don't have to be dragged to Mass every Sunday. I give a lot of credit to the schools for offering those avenues of spiritual growth for our kids to pursue. But they certainly didn't have to pursue them and, believe me, their campuses have plenty of worldly distractions and temptations. There are all kinds of ways they could be spending their time.

When they're home for the summer, they'll sometimes stop in to the chapel to pray. All on their own, with no pushing from us. I think that says a lot right there.

Is the kind of prayer you do before the Blessed Sacrament a different kind of prayer than the prayer you do, say, when you're saying a rosary at home?

Oh, yes. It's more of a one-to-one expression. I find that it's my private time with the Lord, my time to really connect with him. I mean, I pray at other times, too—lots of times, on my way into work in the morning, for example—but it's just more ... being there in the presence of the Lord is enlightening, it's uplifting, it's encouraging; it's all of those kinds of things. You come out and it's almost as if you've been exercising. You often have that mild sense of euphoria that you get when you've been working out. It's the same kind of feeling you have after you've had your special time with Jesus.

It's interesting. The Church has many saints who had very pronounced interior and exterior experiences during adoration—ecstasies, levitations, what have you. And yet it's almost better not to get those kinds of signs and consolations, because without them, you really have to exercise your faith to progress. You can't continue to believe without an act of the will, and that act is less dramatic if all you're doing is responding to sensory stimuli.

I think sometimes people come to a place where they're not altogether whole. They can't seem to get their life together, and they're really having a hard time believing in God. I wonder if God has given us the witness of the people who have had these extraordinary experiences to give those real strugglers something extra to hold on to. You know, it might be the spark that ignites, or reignites, their faith.

Obviously it's possible to develop an unhealthy focus on those kinds of "signs and wonders," as they call them. Because then you're looking to God to put on a magic show, or to do everything for you, to make your relationship with him a one-way street. And that kind of faith really doesn't carry you when the going gets rough. In fact, it often burns itself out rather quickly.

But, then again, why shouldn't God continue to work miracles to inspire faith in him, to remind us that our ways are not his ways? Jesus certainly performed miracles.

One of the really interesting things to me is that people who are steady in their devotion to Jesus in the Eucharist tend not to be the ones chasing the latest popular religious enthusiasm, whatever it happens to be. Whether it's an apparent silhouette of the Blessed Mother in a pane of glass or a Christlike face on a slice of toast, you tend not to find eucharistic adorers chasing those sorts of things around. They are realistic, never starry-eyed. They are even-tempered; their feet are firmly on the ground. And yet these are the same people who are undergoing some fairly profound interior religious experiences. I find that dichotomy very intriguing.

Yes, absolutely. It is contradictory.

You sound like a very down-to-earth, no-nonsense person yourself. And yet there you are, up at four in the morning to go pray and contemplate God in silence.

In some ways, that's why it can get kind of tricky to explain eucharistic adoration to people who are not at all religiously inclined—the people who think you've gone off the deep end and become a religious fanatic when they hear you get up at four in the morning to go into a chapel to pray once a week. They're a little suspicious of that, as if they're afraid of catching something from you. And that something is what they see as an unrealistic outlook on life. They think you're in the same basic place as the people chasing the image of Jesus on the slice of toast.

I also find that there are people I work with and know, and they know that I go to adoration regularly. I don't talk about it all the time in the sense that, you know, it's a private thing. They know I go, and that's OK.

But there is a sense of admiration they have. When people are in crisis or going through health problems or what have you, I might say, very matter-of-factly, "Well, I'm going to adoration on Wednesday; I'll say a prayer for you." And they'll come back later—they always want to tell me what happened.

There's one coworker in particular right now who's having all kinds of health issues going on with people in her family. I asked her the other day, "How did your sister do today?" Her sister had some kind of radical breast cancer surgery, very difficult, and her time is limited; I think they're giving her six months or so. And her sister has decided not to go through radiation, so she's very upset about the whole thing and what it's doing to her family. So she's talked about this a lot to me. I kind of support her when I can.

So, with that situation in mind, I went and did my adoration and I came back. I didn't tell her I was praying for her at all, and she said, "Guess what? My sister is going to go and get the radiation." She had just been hoping so hard that this would happen. Or at least that her sister would try something. I think she had gone into a state of depression worrying about all this.

I said, "That's wonderful news. I've been praying about this, so I'm really glad to hear everything's working out."

And she just looked at me like she was so pleased. And she's a believer anyway, so it's not like that was an issue. But they'll come to you because they're drawn by your devotion. They look at you as, "You're talking to God; can you tell him something for me?"

There are a bunch of people like that within my little circle of family, coworkers and friends, people who know I go to adoration. It's not at all unusual for one of them to ask me to pray for something for them. And it's kind of neat when they come right back to me and tell me something good has happened for them.

And these are not particularly religious people, right?
Right. There are some who have come here to my parish once or twice to pray themselves. I get the feeling that they could very well become involved with eucharistic adoration if their home parish offered it.

How often do you get asked for prayer on someone's behalf?
In the year and a half that I've been going to adoration, I'd say it's been around twenty times or so. And I will mention to them after I've prayed for them that I did so, and then they'll always come to me and ask me again.

So you can see where your relationships are being improved and positively impacted, and where people in your circle are being quietly pointed toward God.

Absolutely. Exactly. And I'm sure that Jay has had similar experiences. People know that you have your faith, they find out about adoration. And that's one more way of witnessing. People are impressed. They say, "You get up that early every week and never miss? Wow." And you don't wear it on your sleeve, you don't say, "Yeah, see how wonderful and holy I am." You just laugh or make a friendly joke about it and let them know by your steadiness that it's an important part of your life. People recognize it as a positive right away.

What other changes have you noticed in your life since you started eucharistic adoration?

Well, you look at all of life that's around you in a different way. That's no exaggeration. I look at all I have instead of what I don't have, and that didn't always come naturally to me.

One of the things I really like to do in adoration is think of all the good things that have happened through my faith in God. All the times I've prayed for something and he's just so clearly come through.

A couple of winters ago, my daughter went on a ski trip. It was to be her first time skiing. As she was getting ready to go, I jokingly said to her, "Break a leg." Well, wouldn't you know it—that's just what she did. It was a very traumatic break. The leg was broken in three places. She had to have a rod and screws implanted, and she really went through a lot with it. She was in the hospital for a week. But all I could think of was, first time skiing—it really could have been much worse. It might have been her head instead of her leg. As life-altering as it is to have a rod in your leg, you can get over it. A lot of people have much worse things happen to them. And my daughter is practically a straight-A student. So I just brought that before the Blessed Sacrament: how blessed we are to have such wonderful kids.

So those kinds of episodes really drive home what eucharistic adoration is all about. If I wasn't going to adoration, I don't know how I would look at these things.

So your time before the Blessed Sacrament is deeply quiet, and it lets you feel God's love.

Yes. But I also think it lets you look around and get down to a level that you can see what you really need. And I mean need, as opposed to what's nice to have. We're surrounded by all these material things, and we're not above all that just because we go to eucharistic adoration, just because we really try to live our Christian faith. We're still tempted by the modern world's comforts, conveniences and diversions. Everybody wants to have nice things for their family. But at the same time, it's easier to sort through that stuff, and separate them from the things that are God-given. You can find beauty in nonmaterialistic things around you that you never much noticed before. Circumstances, people, opportunities to be there for people going through various kinds of struggles.

I mean, you look around and you think, "Do I really need the new clothes, the new car, whatever?" And you find the strength to say, "No, that's not going to make me happy." You can see past the selling, the pitch.

I actually find myself more tuned in to all the natural beauty around me. Not to sound corny, but I mean like in simple leaves on the trees in our yard or the flowers I have in my plants. I find that I appreciate the smaller things like those much more now than I used to. Is that appreciation flowing from my deeper faith, from my time spent with Jesus in eucharistic adoration? I honestly don't know. Maybe it's just me getting older. But I do know that, in my quiet time before the Blessed Sacrament, I thank God for my growing appreciation of these little things; I'm aware of my diminishing appetite for the material things that used to seem so important and irresistible.

God's real presence brings me back to his grace, back to the simple things in life being enough.

CHAPTER 9

Simonetta

"When we come back in the evening we have one hour of adoration before Jesus in the Blessed Sacrament, and [at] this you will be surprised: We have not had to cut down our work for the poor [to allow us time for eucharistic adoration]. The one hour of adoration is the greatest gift God could give a community because ... we love the poor with greater and deeper faith and love."

Mother Teresa of Calcutta (1910–97)

"Aw, come on, Dave. Simonetta's story will add some neat flavor to your book. Do you have any other performing-artist types with a solid reversion story plus links to [a famous priest]?"

So said the e-mail I received days before deadline. It was from a gentleman named Len. We had corresponded weeks prior about the possibility of my calling to get his wife's testimony for my book, but she had fallen ill with the flu. When he finally wrote to say Simonetta was ready to talk, I politely explained that the window had closed on the interview phase of the project.

Well. As I said earlier, I'm a sucker for a good conversion story. And reversions are my favorite kind, since I'm something of a "revert" myself. "OK—you've talked me into it," I wrote back to Len, "even though it's going to mean sweating the deadline for yours truly."

Good move on my part.

Simonetta is a full-time wife and mother, and a talented singer-songwriter on the side. She's also a generous one: She doesn't sell her music—she gives it away for free at her Web site, www.saintphilomena.com. Best of all, her tunes are gems of Catholic devotion—written before the Blessed Sacrament.

In fact, I'm closing with her story because I think her and Len's blossoming ministry is the very embodiment of Pope John Paul II's exhortation to "live the Eucharist" so that from the interior renewal it brings will flow a specific exterior action: experiencing "the joy of witnessing to God's merciful love of the world."

Your husband tells me you're a "revert"—raised Catholic, you left for an evangelical Protestant church, only to return to the Church later on.

I don't think I ever really formally left the Catholic Church, but eventually I wandered far enough from it that I wasn't *in it* in anything but a legal sense. There came a point in my life where the Protestant church became very appealing to me because I had a lack of knowledge of my own, Catholic faith.

"The" Protestant church? You mean a local branch of a large denomination, or an independent, evangelical fellowship?

Well, there were several different churches and ministries that I came in contact with, through different friends and different levels of involvement.

Back up a little further for me, if you would. What period of your life was this? You were raised Catholic ...

Yes. My parents were very devout in the faith. My father was an organist in the church; my mother was a Lithuanian opera singer. I went to

Catholic grade school and Catholic high school. I even went to daily Mass with my father for the first four years of my life. This was before the changes of Vatican II had taken hold and the parish still had daily Mass in Latin.

And then, through high school, there was just the expectation, the duty, that you go to Mass. And I did. But, once I got out of high school, things began to change for me. It was the unawareness of what the Mass was truly about. And then there was confusion, or lack of understanding, about what the Eucharist was.

Then I went to college and continued, more or less, on that same track: dutiful Mass attendance without knowing what was going on.

Did you go to a secular college?
Yes, I did, and one of the interesting things is that I didn't finish college before I got married. I dropped out for a while, and it was in that period that my husband and I got married. And it was interesting because when we got married we thought it would be good to start looking around at churches. I was working as a graphic designer at the time.

What was interesting was that we got married in the Church and still I had no real depth in my understanding of the Eucharist, the Mass, the sacraments. I was just going through the motions and thinking, "This is important, but I don't know why. It really doesn't resonate for me at all." I knew it was important that I get married in the Church and be a good Catholic, but I wasn't getting anything out of it.

Well, maybe I wasn't as in the dark as I make it sound—I had absorbed some of what I had been taught. But I really didn't have a deep understanding of what was going on in the Mass or what the faith was all about.

So after we got married and found a parish, I had met some friends who were not Catholic. And they had started to invite me to their services at an independent evangelical church. Well, I was very intrigued because there was such vibrancy and knowledge of the Bible. These people were applying Scripture to everyday problems and situations.

I was amazed by their biblical knowledge and their intense devotion to Jesus. And I remember one of them telling me, "You're scary if you believe in Mary!" I thought, "Uh-oh."

And all of this started to bring doubt into my life over my Catholic faith. Here I was meeting all these people who seemed to love Jesus so much. It struck me that they had something going with him that I didn't have. I loved Jesus, too, but it wasn't like being *in love* with him the way these people obviously were. Just so excited to talk about him and grow in their faith in him.

How far back was this?

Well, it was not long before our first child was born, which was in 1988. We have four children now.

Was your husband going through the same kind of spiritual search as you were?

Not really. I was the one who was always searching; he kind of went along with me in my search. He's a cradle Catholic, too, and his experiences had been similar to mine. And yet, he always let me know that he disagreed when I said I wanted to make that final step and leave the Catholic Church and formally join an evangelical Protestant church. He'd always play the "Your Father" card. He'd say, "Your father would never stand for it; he'd never speak to us again."

Well, that was successful, but only up to a point. I kind of kept one foot in the door and the other out. And I continued to sort of sample different Protestant churches.

So you never joined an evangelical church, but you were immersed in that culture. Were you reading books, listening to tapes and so on?
All of that. I mean, I was totally immersed in that culture, much more so than in the Catholic culture. And I was very active in a local MOPS group, Mothers of PreSchoolers, which here at least is very evangelical. All my closest friends were evangelicals; we were active in their Bible studies. All of that. I was just very much a part of that without ever formally joining a congregation.

And yet, come Sunday morning, we continued to go to Mass. Actually, I'm thinking back now, there was a period where I quit going to Mass, but my husband never quit even though he went along with me on my evangelical excursions. I quit going because I felt I didn't need to anymore. One of the things my evangelical friends had convinced me of was that the early Christians simply prayed wherever they were; come the Lord's Day, it was fine to just pray right there in your own home. Church was good because you needed fellowship for encouragement and preaching for growth, but it was really optional. No big deal if you didn't make it.

I don't think it was until after we had our children that I had some conflicts with some of the things that were being said. I remember we had a women's Bible group and one of the women had just lost her mother. She was crying, and she said, "I don't think my mother was saved." And they were all saying, "Oh, that's so sad." They really had no ray of hope they could offer her.

I knew there was something a little off about that, so I said to this girl, "Can't you pray for her?" And they all just about jumped right down my throat. They said, "No, she can't. Her mother is gone. If she didn't get saved while she had a chance, it's too late now." And of course they were quoting the Bible to back up what they were saying.

So that was one of the first things that started to tip me off to the fact that some of their interpretations of the Bible were very simplistic and kind of novel. As other similar kinds of conflicts arose, I realized that I had some things embedded in my soul that I couldn't be swayed from. Things I knew to be true even if I couldn't argue as passionately or rattle off as many verses of Scripture for the situation as spontaneously as they could.

So, of course, the more they saw that I wasn't being persuaded by their arguments, the more insistent they became, the more they sought to undo my "Catholic thinking." And as those kinds of situations started to grow in frequency, I started to see them as red flags.

And another thing, one of the biggest things, was the way they talked about communion. They had a little wafer that they would eat kind of ceremoniously, but they said it was just a representation of Jesus, a remembrance of the Last Supper. And again, they backed up their point of view on it with Scripture verses. *Selective* Scripture verses. And that really caught my attention. I knew they were quite a ways off on that one.

It sounds like you were in the same place G.K. Chesterton was in when he was investigating Christianity and mulling conversion. Looking back on the process after he had become a Catholic, he said, "I never dreamed that the Roman religion was true; but I knew that its accusers, for some reason or other, were curiously inaccurate."

I recognize that element in your testimony myself, because I hit

the same spot after I had embraced evangelical Protestantism. Like you, I was raised Catholic but drifted away from the Church after Confirmation. Far away from Christ altogether, in fact. And yet, I feel like I have to give credit where it's due whenever I talk about this: I probably wouldn't be here talking to you right now if not for the witness of evangelical Protestants who really presented the Gospel to me in a way that made me sit up, listen and "make a decision for Christ." But, gradually, the inaccuracies of the things they said about the Catholic Church, things I knew were not right but they taught as gospel truth, caused me to look into how the Church gave account of itself, rather than only getting the story from their one, obviously biased, side.

Yeah, that's just about exactly it. Another big part of it for me was their attacks on Mary. I thought, "How can they be so hateful toward the Mother of Our Lord?" They seemed very afraid to acknowledge her, even though she's right there in the Bible saying that "all generations shall call me blessed." There were so many of these red flags that I just said, "How can I immerse myself into this faith when there seems to be so much askew with it?"

For me, it was there that God really started turning the lights on. I was in the midst of this fairly intense search for him in various churches and Bible studies and fellowship groups. And it was just very clear to me that he was saying, "If you want to keep seeking, that's fine; go right ahead. But don't completely shut out the Catholic Church. Keep it in the mix of churches you're looking into."

I guess the final straw was when it came time to start schooling our children. I was starting to bring them to Bible studies and all these other groups. I remember asking my husband, "We need to decide what we're going to teach our children. Are we going to give them a

Christian upbringing and not have anything to do with the Mass? Or are we going to teach them about the Mass?"

My husband said, very firmly: "We need to teach them about the Mass." And I knew he was right. So as we moved ahead with that, I started to meet Catholic women through a home-school group. And the first meeting that I went to was a shocker. All these women, young women for the most part, knelt down and said a rosary before they started the meeting. And I was so stubborn. I sat in my chair and I refused to pray. I thought, "How fanatical these women are! How rude that they expect me to just fall in line and pray with them—to Mary, no less." I actually felt offended. [Laughs.]

So for a while I remained resistant to Catholic devotions like that. I couldn't bring myself to give in, with all I had heard in my years with evangelical Protestants.

I remember talking to a friend of mine. I said, "I'm teaching the girls about the Catholic faith, but I'm really struggling. I'm struggling with Mary, and a lot of other things, too." She just said one thing and it really seemed to cut to the heart of the matter. She said, "Simonetta, how in the world could you ever give up the Eucharist? Protestants have a remembrance. As Catholics, we have the body and blood, soul and divinity of Christ."

It was like someone had hit me in the head with a brick. I realized what I had forgotten. All at once it was like, "How did I forget that? How did I ever lose sight of it?" And now, today, I see so many Catholics blindly receiving Communion. It's just complete ignorance, like I had. You know they just haven't been touched or reminded, or whatever it takes to get you to realize what the Eucharist really is.

Well, from that moment on, I became more open to the faith. All of a sudden, I realized: The Eucharist isn't just another issue to be considered along with all the other issues. It isn't just something that different Christians do in different ways. It's the central truth that defines us as Catholics. It's not something *about* the Catholic faith—it *is* the Catholic faith. It's Jesus.

How long ago was it that this all fell into place for you?
Six years ago. It was seven years ago that I started Catholic home-schooling, and a year into that that this friend turned the lights on about the Eucharist for me.

Looking back, if that moment had not happened, I probably would not have ventured to go on any Catholic retreats. Her witness really set me up for this four-day retreat that I was thinking about going on at the time. It was going to be with Father John Hardon, who has since died. People in my new Catholic circle had been talking about how wonderful his retreats were, what good spiritual direction he gave, how enlightening his talks were. And I knew I was ripe for that from the Catholic Church. I knew I needed to make a move one way or the other on the Church and find out something deeper.

So this was the move I made. I went on this retreat with Father Hardon. And, you know, in retrospect, the evil one kept trying to keep me from going on that retreat. He tried so hard. I got sick the day I was to drive to the retreat house; I suddenly got the worst flu. I had somewhat of a fever, and that made me even more apprehensive about going and being with all these Catholic women. I was like, "Oh, no—it's going to be just me alone with all of them!" [Laughs.] And it was to be a silent retreat, which made me all the more nervous. I started to drag my feet a little, and my husband stepped in and encouraged me; he said, "You really should go; I have a feeling you're going to get a lot out of it." So I sort of forced myself to go. Then, on the way to the retreat house, we got lost and the car broke down.

In retrospect, seeing what happened on that very retreat, and in the months and years since then, it's so clear that the evil one did not want me on that retreat.

What happened on the retreat?
That was really the beginning of my Catholic faith really catching fire.

Because of something you heard there?
Not so much because of what I heard, no. It was really two things. One was, when I got there, they had a signup sheet for Father Hardon. You probably know who he is, don't you?

Oh, yes. He was a very solid Jesuit theologian. He died recently and left behind a tremendous body of work.
Right. Well, he was also a very popular spiritual director around here. People would be dying to talk to him for spiritual direction. It was very hard to get time with him on his retreats because everyone wanted to get in to talk to him.

On this first Catholic retreat I went on, there was a signup sheet. And it was fifteen minutes per person; there were so many people that that was all you could get. Well, when I got to that sheet, because I was late—because of the car problems and getting lost and being sick—it was completely booked up. I just said, "Oh, well. That's the way that goes." And there was another priest giving spiritual direction, so I think I was about to sign up on his sheet.

All of a sudden a woman came up to me. She was handicapped; she could barely walk. She saw me standing there, looking at the charts, and she asked me: "Did you want to see Father Hardon?" And I said,

"I've heard he's very good; I was kind of hoping to meet with him." So she said, "I'll give you half of my time."

Now, that was rare. Because when people go on these retreats, they sign up for four days, and the main draw is whatever little time they can get one to one with the spiritual director. Especially a very popular one like Father Hardon.

Well, she said her time was at 10:30 and that I should be there, at the door, at 10:35. I thought she meant 10:35 in the morning—I was still feeling ill and really not thinking straight. So later that evening I was sitting out in the library enjoying the quiet, reading, and here she comes, hobbling quickly over to me; you could hear her coming from a long way off. And she said, "Are you nuts? Did you know you're giving up your seven and a half minutes with Father Hardon?"

So I ran down the hall and into the room with Father Hardon. I introduced myself, we spoke for several minutes and then I asked him, "Father, do we all need a spiritual director?" He said, "No. My spiritual director is my journal. God is my director." He said, "Trust me; you need to write, and write and write some more. God will talk to you through your journaling. Spend time before the Eucharist, and write."

I said, "Father, I don't really like to write. I'm not very good at it. I'm not especially articulate; I really struggle when I need to write something. I just don't think that's my calling."

He said: "Write." He said, "There's a woman who told me the same thing you just said two years ago. She just had a book published of her writings."

I just said, "OK; thank you, Father." And that was that. But I was really intrigued with his story about the lady who didn't want to write and ended up writing a book. Well, I went to Confession that same night, with a different priest, and for penance he asked me, "Do you know what a holy hour is?" I said, "No." I had no idea what one was. He said, "Spend an hour in front of Jesus in the Eucharist, and pray. And what I also want you to do is write before the Blessed Sacrament."

So here two different priests have given me the same "prescription" within a few hours of each other. I thought, "Well, I guess I'm going to write in front of the Eucharist!" Off to the retreat house chapel I went. They had eucharistic adoration there, something I had hardly noticed before. And that was the night I saw Jesus in the Eucharist— not visibly, but in the sense of experiencing him for who he is, and really being in his presence.

I cried for the entire hour. I knew he was really present. And I wrote and I wrote and I wrote.

How did you know Jesus was really present?
Hmm. I'll try to explain it.

I knew Jesus was there because I felt this great love. And it was feeling this great love from him that brought me to tears, because I saw myself in a way—in all the difficulties I had been going through on my spiritual search, the doubting, the despair—I just had the warm sense of his love. That's probably the best I can do to describe it.

And then, feeling that intense sense of his love, I actually got the *urge* to write. Yes, I was following the two priests' direction, but it went way beyond that. I was moved just to write about my life, and different ways that God had been apparent in my life. Plus different things that I had done. It was probably very much like a life confession, or a general confession, I guess you call it. And I could sense within me, and outside of myself, very clearly, the presence of pure, powerful love. And with this unexplainable love, I could feel God's grace flowing into my heart and mind. I knew I was being refreshed and renewed in a way I never had been before.

I was sitting way in the back of this pretty big chapel, and I had such a strong desire to go way up to the front, right up close to the exposed Eucharist. There was a woman up there, and several others in the pews, and I had a sense of apprehension. I was somewhat fearful. But I couldn't stop hearing in my heart: "That's God." And that just made me want to get up much closer to him, as if being physically closer would bring me closer to him in the larger spiritual sense.

So I walked up and knelt on the kneeler that was right up next to the altar on which the Host was exposed.

What was your initial response when you got there?
I remember that it was very late at night, very still and quiet. And I just stared into the Host. It was almost as if I was seeing someone for the first time after getting to know him over a long period of time through correspondence.

That's a vivid description.
Yeah, I couldn't take my eyes off the Eucharist. I couldn't believe the warmth that I felt, this ineffable love. I had just never experienced anything like that before, really. I thought, "Where was I, through my whole life, that I never experienced this? How is it that I never knew that God was here all along, in this very special way, and I was so blocked from him?"

So, from that moment, I began to spend time in eucharistic adoration. And I began to write while in adoration. And it was through my writing that the songs began to form, without my ever setting out to write songs per se. They just came.

How often do you go to adoration?

Well, it varies now. For a while, my husband's job allowed us to go to daily Mass as a family, and the church we went to had adoration after Mass every day. There were many times where my husband's schedule worked out so that he would meet me at church. After Mass, he would take the children out to the playground nearby while I went in to adoration for a half hour; then he'd come in to adoration and I would take the kids. And sometimes the kids would stay with us in adoration. Other times he would take the kids home and I would just stay there, praying and writing for hours.

Your husband must have been thrilled that you came home to the Church so strongly.

He was. My experiences helped awaken his faith, I'm sure. He didn't have the resistance to the Church that I had, but he definitely needed to be awakened to God's love at work in his life.

And, for you, the songs came, one after the next.

The words seemed to be coming from Jesus—not like a direct inspiration like the writers of Scripture had, by any means, but in the form of a growing understanding that I just had to find a way to put into words.

Why songs? Why not straight prose, or even poetry?

Well, I played the guitar years before. I had stopped playing because I had a falling-out with my sisters years and years ago. They were a trio, and they had another girl come into their group, and it wasn't me. [Laughs.] And I was somewhat offended. But God had a plan, because they weren't singing particularly edifying music, let alone Christian music. They were singing in lounges and places like that. So that could have been a bad road for me to go down. God had other plans for me, I guess.

You didn't set out to write songs in your journal, though, did you? You just wanted to record your experiences in adoration, right?
Yeah. How did I end up writing songs? I don't know. I truly don't.

The funny thing is, the first song I wrote, I remember I was struggling so hard at the time. We had just left church, after Mass and adoration. On the way home, we stopped at an ice cream place and my husband said, "Don't forget what Father always says: Keep your eyes on the Beloved." So we get back in the car and, as we're driving home, I start humming a tune that fits those words. And suddenly the next line comes to me, along with a melody. "Keep your eyes on the Beloved/He will bring you everlasting peace." So I sang it to myself, right there in the car as it came to me. When I got home, I was singing it quietly and my husband asked me what I was singing. I said, "Oh, something that just came to me." He said, "That's pretty good. You need to finish it."

So, during my writing time in adoration, I did just that. I wrote out a song around that first line. The words just kind of came to me. So that's how my first song came about, and after that they just seemed to flow one after the other.

I remember speaking with my spiritual director while on retreat about that time. I was going through a very difficult time and I said, "I'm very angry, but I've written a song—and I don't even write music!" He said, "I want to hear this song." So I sang the song for him and he said, "That's beautiful. I really loved it. You should keep writing songs—I think God has something in store for you there."

Were songs ever the only thing you were writing down in your journal?

No, never. I also just recorded my experiences, plus at various times I was doing spiritual exercises, such as the Ignatian exercises (created by St. Ignatius of Loyola, founder of the Society of Jesus, also known as the Jesuits), which take you through daily meditations. So a big part of what I recorded then, for instance, was my daily dialogue with God through these meditations.

And when that was through, I went through St. Francis de Sales' *Introduction to the Devout Life*, recording my experiences with that book. And there were other books I used to guide me as well, writing my thoughts about how God touched me through the writings and the exercises. And in writing about what they meant to me, a song would come. Sometimes it seemed like one song would lead almost directly to another.

Through it all, I came to appreciate that the driving force behind the whole process was Jesus in the Eucharist. And I came to see that God was using me as a tool to write these songs.

Now, there's a danger in thinking that you've got a direct pipeline to the mind of God. And yet, I remember one time, I read a line to my husband and his reaction was, "I don't know exactly how, but I think that's theologically unsound." This was on about my seventh song, and this was the first time he had stopped me like that. So it was really disturbing to me. I thought, "Boy, how did I feel so strongly about this phrase and yet it's an error?"

Well, we went to Mass that night. And would you believe that the Gospel reading was about my very phrase! It directly answered my husband's doubt on that phrase; there it was, in almost the exact same words, in Scripture. And read at Mass just a few hours after we had talked about it. My husband turned to me and said, "You were right after all."

Again, I didn't take this to mean that I was suddenly empowered by God to write infallibly or anything like that. Nothing like that. But I definitely saw it as a clear sign that God wanted me to continue to write before the Eucharist. And it showed me how powerful—how *powerful*—it is to be before him. It showed me that he is really present in the Eucharist. And it showed me that I shouldn't keep this to myself; I should continue to write songs as a way to share Jesus with others, a way to point other people to his love for them.

Do you perform live?

Yes, but not as much as most professional Catholic musicians. And the reason is, I'm homeschooling my children. All four of them. And I was homeschooling before all this—I knew I was called to homeschool, because, when I was finishing my bachelor's degree, I heard a woman talking about homeschooling on "Focus on the Family," which is an evangelical Protestant radio program. When I heard this woman talk about her experiences homeschooling her daughter, God opened my heart to the idea instantly. I just knew it's what he wanted me to do. I decided right then and there to give up my aspiration for an advanced degree in order to homeschool my children.

So, when the music ministry began, I knew God wasn't calling me to give up homeschooling; he wanted me to do both. I could see the importance of teaching my children the depth of the faith, having lost the faith myself, or never really getting it, even after attending Catholic schools.

So, because homeschooling takes priority over the music ministry, most of the performing takes place in the Midwest, with some longer trips planned in bunches to limit the impact on my family. For the most part, though, I'm not able to travel very far from home.

But you've cut a CD—that allows you to reach people well beyond your immediate area.

Yes. God has really been good to me. There's the CD, which has been distributed in all fifty states and many foreign countries, and I have a book on tape that's been quite well received. Plus I've been a guest on several EWTN programs, which reach more people than I would be able to even if I toured all the time.

And you give your CDs away for free. How, if you don't mind my asking, are you able to afford that?

Well ... God! Mother Teresa always said that God has plenty of money. And it's true. When I started recording, we were paying out of our own pockets for the studio time, the professional arranger and all the related expenses. It's very expensive. Halfway through the tracks, I started a novena to St. Philomena. And there was this woman who was a doctor, sixty-two years old. Instead of retiring, she had decided to go into a cloistered monastery. She became our first benefactor. She donated enough money to what we named the Saint Philomena Foundation to cover the entire recording process, the replicating, everything we had to do to run off a supply of CDs and cassettes.

Meanwhile, while God is doing all this through your songwriting, what has been the effect on your prayer life, your personal relationship with Jesus, through eucharistic adoration?

Well, I can't really separate the two because the songs come from my relationship with Jesus. They're like my love songs to him. And the

164

other journaling I do in adoration, the other prayer—it's all part of the same process. Which is growing in faith, hope and love in Christ.

Nearly every other person I've interviewed has described going through a period of dryness in their prayer life after the "honeymoon" phase faded into routine. Did you experience that?

Oh, did I ever. I think all souls seeking after God go through it.

I had bouts of despair while going through the dry times, and I thought maybe I was doing something wrong. And part of the dryness in prayer and devotion was dryness in songwriting. The songs sort of stopped coming. I wondered what I might be doing wrong, but then I came to realize, through my reading of Scripture and spiritual guidance books, that dryness and darkness—the nagging sense that God isn't there anymore—is the most important source of grace there is in adoration.

I've just recorded a book on tape, *King of the Golden City*; I did the voices of the characters. There's a chapter in the book, which was written by a nun, called "Brave Love." And what this chapter is about is going through the dryness, going through the darkness, and not feeling God's presence, but persevering through it all.

In this chapter, the little girl asks Jesus: "How come all of a sudden I don't feel like praying to you? How come I don't feel like spending time with you? Am I doing something wrong that has caused me to lose my warm affection for you?" And Jesus answers: "You used to come to me to see what I had in my hands for you. Now you come just to look at my face. Which do you think is better?"

For me, that was just so beautiful and so right on with what I was going through when I first read it. Coming to Jesus and always looking for what he can give us—good feelings, affirmations, consolations—really doesn't help us progress in faith, hope and love. I've really come to appreciate that since going through a lot of dryness, and staying there.

My husband said to me one time, "Simonetta, you may have done the Ignatian spiritual exercises, but your charism really isn't like St. Ignatius'; it's much more like that of St. Thérèse of the Child Jesus, the Little Flower." And he was right—I identify with the spirituality of Thérèse and also the other great Carmelites, Sts. Teresa of Avila and John of the Cross. They knew, and they said it so profoundly and so beautifully, that we can't stay long at that consolation level and expect to grow. You almost welcome the darkness and the dryness, even though you might not enjoy it on the sensory, feeling level, because you know that, by it, you will grow much deeper in Christ.

There were days where there was darkness and not wanting to pray—going to daily Mass was difficult, praying was difficult, eucharistic adoration was difficult. Everything related to my walk with God just felt like a chore. There would be days where I would sit before the exposed Blessed Sacrament and say, "Here I am before you, Jesus; where are you?" [Laughs.]

Through all of this, I gradually learned that Jesus was there and, in fact, that he was especially consoled by my coming to be with him at the times when I was getting so little in return. Because it was at those times that I was making a sacrifice to be there; I was there for him out of love, not my own need. You always make sacrifices for the ones you love; that's really a big part of what love is. Also, Jesus loves when we trust him, and my trust had to be stronger in those times.

Probably the most concise way to explain it is to say that it went from being about me to being about him. There was a fundamental switch in the equation of who is getting what.

I've talked with close to twenty people while researching this book, and just about everyone has described the same stages you just did. It's interesting how closely eucharistic life in Christ resembles the progression of a normal, healthy marriage—there's a honeymoon phase, a letdown, sometimes quite disconcerting, and then a leveling off into a stable, committed, trusting, intimate bond.

Boy, that's so true. The first six months or so after that retreat with Father Hardon, my life in Christ felt so incredibly intense, especially when I was with Jesus in eucharistic adoration. And I underline the word "felt." But, having gone through these other stages, I believe that was because *I* was so very intense emotionally during that phase. I was just spending so many hours in adoration, working through so many spiritual and doctrinal issues and going through so many emotions and feelings. And now, with both that and the really low dry spells all behind me, there's a quality to my life in Christ—I guess *maturity* is the right word for it—that I probably could not have imagined back then.

Three years ago, I prayed before the Blessed Sacrament for three hours at a spell. But what was it all about? I think it was about my neediness. And it's funny, because God doesn't allow me the luxury of that many hours with him in adoration anymore. Our schedules don't allow it. It's like God let me have just what I needed, just when I needed it—and now he's calling me to something more, something of better quality and greater maturity.

How much time do you spend in adoration now?

At least an hour a week, but it's not like it's always an hour at a shot. Sometimes it's three or four shorter visits. There are three churches in our area that have adoration, one of them perpetual. We've been taking our children at least once a week to make a holy hour, as a family, after Sunday Mass.

Do your children seem to enjoy sitting in silence for an hour before the Blessed Sacrament?

Well, they range in age from four to thirteen, and I don't know if "enjoy" is quite the right word. I think they see it as part of who they are, because it's been a part of their lives for most of their lives. The four-year-old—we always hope she'll fall asleep. [Laughs.] One of the neat things is that my oldest two like to pray the Stations of the Cross out in the main sanctuary. And, of course, the younger ones want to be wherever the older ones are. There's another family at that church with kids around the same age, so the parents will sit in adoration while the children are doing the Stations, usually with one of the parents.

Is dryness something to get past or something you learn to live with because, once it's on you, it never goes away completely? Or, at least, isn't that sort of what Teresa of Avila said, that dryness is a fact of the spiritual life?

I don't think that's quite what she said; nor do I think St. John of the Cross said the dark night of the soul is a permanent state. In fact, they both talked about emerging from the dark night with a heart burning for love of God. It's just that the fire isn't a raging inferno so much as a steady, eternal flame.

For me, right now, the dry spells come and go. When you ask this question, I think of one retreat I was on, recently, where I was in adoration and I wrote, "What do I hear when I hear your voice?" I was looking right at the Eucharist. And I said, "Well? What *do* I hear?" I tried turning it back over to Jesus. I said, "I don't know what to write here—please tell me!" [Laughs.] And the words came to me: "What I hear is your love."

When I wrote down those words, the Holy Spirit just filled me. I came to tears. And I realized that you don't "hear love" through the ears, but through the heart. It came to me that we're looking for love sometimes not so much in the wrong places, but we're going about looking in the wrong way. I just kind of got it at that moment that the heart is the organ that hears the voice of God's love. I think I got it because it was happening to me right there and then: My heart heard the voice of his love.

Didn't St. Thérèse of Lisieux fall into terrible despair for a time? In a way, she never came out of the dark night, once she entered into it, until she died.

Well, I think that's true. The sense that God had abandoned her enveloped her when she was in the latter stages of her suffering with tuberculosis; she became utterly despondent. But she persevered with such love. She was relentless in her love for God even when she felt totally alienated from him. She was only twenty-four when she died; had she survived the disease and recovered, maybe she would have come out of the dark night. Who knows? She was one of the holiest souls who ever lived. She was obviously rewarded for her persevering love—we know that she went straight to heaven. And, of course, she had tremendous devotion to the Eucharist.

Do you think there's any danger of treating eucharistic adoration as a kind of transcendental meditation? It's very tempting to read, for example, Teresa of Avila, who was so advanced in prayer, and want

**to skip all the steps it took her to get there—Scripture study, cat-
echesis, studying the teachings of the Church—and just go and sit
in silence with Jesus hour after hour. I wonder if adoration in a
vacuum doesn't become, for some people, an inadvertent stumble
into New Ageism and such. What do you think?**

Well, that's interesting. I never really gave that a lot of thought. I think
I naively came to the conclusion that everyone would feel as I do, that
it was because of ignorance that I didn't understand that the Eucharist
is Jesus really present. And my hunger for more understanding
launched me into the journaling, which launched me into reading the
solid meat of the faith—Scripture, catechetics, the writings of the
Church's established spiritual masters. The more I read, the more I
learned, the deeper I went, the more alive the Eucharist came for me.
And the more I just kept growing.

I can't imagine somebody just sitting before the Eucharist and
expecting to be infused by the Holy Spirit with knowledge and understanding of what's going on.

I do know that sometimes we're called to just be still with God.
There are no words; you just need to *be* before Jesus. But if that's all
you ever did, you would certainly hit a dead end. It's just one way God
reaches out to us; if you made it the only way you would open yourself to him, it would burn itself out fairly quickly.

I guess I didn't mention it earlier, but reading is just as important a
part of my adoration time as praying and journaling. And, in fact, one
of the things I've learned is that you need to make sure that, when you
do read, you read material that God wants you to read at that particular point in time. I try to rely on my spiritual director to point me to
what I need at any given time. Number one, there's a lot of iffy doctrine out there, unfortunately, even in Catholic bookstores; and,

number two, sometimes you can waste time reading the right material but at the wrong time for you. A good spiritual director can be a godsend in selecting the right material for exactly where you are at any given time in your walk with God.

Could you imagine what your life would be like right now if you didn't have eucharistic adoration as a key dimension of your life in Christ?

Yes, I could, because I think about it often. I think back to the time right before I committed myself to the Catholic faith; I think of the difference between what I was like then—what did I feel like, what condition was my soul in, what was in my heart?—and I think back and say, "I was so shallow." It felt so empty. I remember very well not feeling complete. I knew I was still searching, but I didn't know what I was searching for until I found it. Until I found him, I mean. I knew I was searching for answers to all my spiritual questions, but I didn't know where I was going to find them. And, of course, for a very long time, I never expected to find them in the Catholic Church. There was an emptiness in my soul, and the Eucharist filled it to overflowing.

Editor's note: For more information on Simonetta, or to request her free, award-nominated recordings, write The Saint Philomena Foundation, Suite 140, 15774 S. La Grange Rd., Orland Park, IL 60462. Or visit www.saintphilomena.com on the Internet.

CONCLUSION

Come to the Table

"Could you not keep watch with me for one hour?"

Jesus Christ, ca. 33 A.D.

There you have it. A Catholic journalist went looking for a few good Catholics and got more than he bargained for. And you've just shared in the journey.

Now what?

I sincerely hope and pray that, in hearing these first-person accounts of ordinary folks living lives of extraordinary closeness to Christ, you too will be moved to give Jesus a chance to work in your life through eucharistic adoration.

Where to go to meet our Lord in his humanity as well as his divinity? If you don't know of a church or chapel in your area that offers adoration, contact the Real Presence Eucharistic Education and Adoration Association. This group maintains a state-by-state adoration directory on the Internet at www.therealpresence.org. If you don't have access to an online computer, you can call the association at (773) 586-7809.

If you find that there are no adoration opportunities near you, you can still visit with Jesus. While the term "eucharistic adoration" is formally used to describe prayer before the exposed Host, you can obtain the exact same graces and spiritual benefits by visiting the Lord wherever the Blessed Sacrament is reserved in a tabernacle. And that's the case in nearly every Catholic church. If there's a red or white vigil candle burning near what usually looks like an ornately decorated bread box, Jesus is physically present.

In fact, for me personally, it was by praying before the Blessed Sacrament reserved in a tabernacle in a nearby parish church, just a few minutes of my lunch break each weekday, that I heard God prompting me, quietly but firmly, to leave my job in the secular media for a position in the Catholic press.

No matter how you choose to spend your time with Jesus while you sit with him, be assured that, over time, if you are faithful in your visits, your life will change. *You* will change.

As you do, you may find it helpful to know that, in adoration, you're practicing an ancient form of devotion known as "contemplative prayer." This the *Catechism* defines as "a communion in which the Holy Trinity conforms man, the image of God, to his likeness."

Among eucharistic adorers, the story is often told of St. John Vianney, the small, humble and holy pastor of a country parish in Ars, France, in the 1800s. Father Vianney, who would come to be known as the Curé of Ars, used to watch a farmer coming into the church after working the fields late each afternoon. Day after day, the farmer would kneel and pray before the Blessed Sacrament. Finally Father Vianney, eager to progress in his own prayer life, asked the farmer what it was that he was saying to God each day.

"Oh, I don't say anything," the farmer told him. "I look at him, and he looks at me."

That's contemplative prayer. That's eucharistic adoration. That's interior transformation.

And that's love—the most essential personal project you can take upon yourself if you're serious about pitching in to help build the kingdom of God.

I hope to see you there.

A Prayer Before the Blessed Sacrament

I confess that you, Jesus, are the Christ, the Son of the Living
God.

(see Matthew 16:16)

You have counseled me through the Scriptures:
"Fear not, for I have redeemed you;
I have called you by name: You are mine."

(see Isaiah 43:1)

Lord Jesus Christ, have mercy on me, for I am a sinner.

(see Luke 5:8)

+ + +

Thank you, Jesus; I trust in you.
I trust in your mercy, your love,
your kindness and your compassion for me.

St. Faustina

Jesus, you are my Lord and my God, and I believe in you.

(see John 20:28)

Please, Lord, heal my unbelief.

(see Mark 9:24)